NOTHING SHORT OF A MIRACLE

A Chronicle of a Head Injury Survivor

by

Michael A. Peake

With Linda Blachly

ANDREW PUBLICATIONS
7542 Newberry Lane
Lanham, MD   20706

TABLE OF CONTENTS

INTRODUCTION

It has been five years since I suffered a severe brain stem injury in a near fatal car accident at the age of 19. Stricken down in my early years of adulthood, I was in a coma for nearly four months.

Since waking up, I have had to fight to relearn even the simplest movements. Through therapy nearly every day I went from moving my thumb on command to being able to maneuver myself in bed.

I have had to relearn steps, taken from my childhood to adulthood, but not beginning in a child's body this time. I have had to grow up physically, emotionally and spiritually all over again. I have relearned to do things that an infant has no trouble doing. I then progressed to independently eating and using a wheelchair, and then a single-point cane. In my speech, I went from being able to spell out what I wanted to say to finally being able to say phrases and sentences.

It has been a long journey and I am still traveling along the road of recovery. But, along the way God has been with my family and me every step of this untrod path. He sustained my life when the doctors gave me no hope. He has upheld my parents, family and friends during a time when they had nothing else to cling to.

After I woke up from my coma, God has miraculously intervened to give me the strength, faith and hope to carry on each day. He continues to be my portion every day as I progress or have a setback in my recovery.

The steps that I now take at age 24, the pitfalls He carries me through, the milestones I achieve in my life along this path, are NOTHING SHORT OF A MIRACLE.

Michael A. Peake

ACKNOWLEDGEMENTS

My gratitude goes primarily to the Lord for His inspiration for the writing of this story. Special thanks go to Linda Blachly for all of her editing.

All of the support that I received from family, friends and Pastor Ferguson and his wife is still a very important part of my recovery. Their visitation to me in the hospital while I was in a coma, then after I had awakened, and all of the get well cards given to me are well appreciated. Most importantly, their prayers of support for me and my family were and continue to be a source of strength for us.

There were *many* other caring people showing their support by taking time from their daily schedules to call us or pay a visit. Special gratitude goes to my mom for her continuous love and care given to me.

Michael A. Peake

I thank the Lord for the privilege of helping Mike put this book together. I count it a blessing to have gotten to know Mike and his family better through working on this book, and to be used of God for such a worthy project.

My family had only been members of Trinity Assembly of God in Lanham, Maryland, for nine months when I received the devastating prayer chain phone call on the night of June 16, 1988 — Mike Peake had been involved in an automobile accident and was not expected to live.

I had to struggle to recall exactly what he looked like, since we hadn't been members very long. I knew he was a member of the youth group — that's about all. Then I recalled seeing him and his family in church, although I didn't know them very well.

It didn't matter — they were part of our church family and I cried as I prayed for Mike and his family. Never before in my Christian life had tragedy struck so close to home, and never before had I seen a church come together in prayer so intensely. We clung to reports of his recovery week after week, alternately with waves of sadness and hope and faith.

After almost four months, Mike came out of his coma. Now our prayers turned to recovery. Each week, it seemed, there was hope — God was answering our prayers on Mike's behalf.

The first time we saw Mike back at church — nine months after the accident — was the most emotion-filled moment I have ever felt as I saw him being taken out of the car and put in his wheelchair to come into the church.

Throughout his recovery, however, the thing that ministered to me the most was the dedication of Mike's family and how they rallied around him. This tragedy would have torn up even the most stable of families, but in the Peake family their faith was played out as they drew strength and peace from the Word of God and the church.

Every now and then, along our Christian walk, we meet those who really exemplify Christ in their lives. I think the Peake family — Mike, Marcia, Phil, Karen and Mike Kogok, will never know until eternity the impact they made on other people's lives. That's why this story has been written — to encourage and build up others who might be struggling and to point them to Jesus, our healer, our strength, our peace.

Linda J. Blachly

ENDORSEMENTS

"Being a fellow head injury survivor and a member of the Maryland Head Injury Foundation Board of Directors, I read *Nothing Short of a Miracle: A Chronicle of a Head Injury Survivor* with great personal interest. Michael's vivid recounting of his accident, subsequent acute medical care, in-patient rehabilitation, and faith certainly struck a familiar chord within me.

"I found the book to be accurate, informative and very readable and I would recommend it to persons suffering severe tragedies or to their families. Modern medicine is a miracle in and of itself, but Michael's message of faith and his refusal to give up hope and his subsequent recovery is both inspirational and worthwhile."

Al Bahr
Maryland Head Injury Foundation
Board of Directors

"I was excited to read *Nothing Short of a Miracle: A Chronicle of a Head Injury Survivor* because it is the first book I have seen that documents God's miraculous work in the recovery and rehabilitation of a head injury survivor.

"Each head injury is different, so each of our stories is different. But for all of us, God is more than sufficient. As in Michael's story, God performs miracle after miracle in the life of His children who experience head injury; and he proves Himself faithful over and over, even when our trust in Him wavers.

"This is a book everyone should read. If you don't know a head injury survivor yet, you probably will sometime. And if you don't, Michael's story gives valuable insights about responding to any kind of suffering.

"You'll see clear examples of how God comes through in both big and small ways to lighten our load and to reassure us of His love and care. You will also see through Michael's interaction with family, friends, and health care professionals how God can use each of us to inspire and encourage others.

"Life after a head injury sometimes seems like hell on earth, but God is always there with us and for us. Michael shows us that if we trust God for miracles, we will find them. No matter what we have to face on earth, if we know Jesus as our Savior and Lord as Michael does, we are more than conquerors through Him."

Phyllis King, Ph.D.
Founder and compiler
More Than Survivors:
Head Injury from a Christian Perspective
A monthly support newsletter

CHAPTER 1

Brief Awakening

When I opened my eyes I had no idea where I was or why I was there. There was no one around to give me the details and I made no attempt to find them out. I scanned the room for a clue, and my eyes came to rest on a board with the following message written on it:

God Bless You Michael and welcome to Bryn Mawr Rehabilitation Hospital.
Today is ? , October ? , 1988.

I began to wonder, "*Where in the world is Bryn Mawr?*" and "*What am I doing in a hospital?*" Surprisingly, it didn't even phase me that I couldn't move *at all.* I fell asleep after that.

Little did I realize as I gradually awoke from a coma on that cool October morning, my life as both an active youth leader at my church, Trinity Assembly of God in Lanham, Maryland, and a freshman at the University of Maryland, College Park campus, would never be the same. As a result of a near-fatal car accident on June 16, 1988, I had slept the entire summer away. Now, as the leaves changed color and began to fall, the prognosis that the doctors gave of living like a vegetable for the rest of my life was not promising. Quite a change from the plans and dreams I held as I entered college. I would know nothing of all this for a significant amount of time.

Growing Up

I grew up in Lanham, Maryland, a suburb of Washington, D.C. My mom and dad, Marcia and Phil Peake, and my sister Karen and I were a happy, church-going family. I had always been outgoing and fun-loving, and as I got older, I became more serious about life.

The years 1986-88 had been some of the most important years of my life. It was during those years that I grew academically and socially. The latter stages of my physical growth didn't occur until after 1986. I was voted one of the two shortest kids in my senior class (1986-87) of Parkdale High School.

I received academic awards when I graduated high school in the spring of 1987. They were: The Presidential Academic Achievement Award, The State of Maryland Merit Scholastic Award, The Kiwanis Club Citizenship Award, and I was inducted into the National Honor Society. From 1987-88 I completed my freshman year at the University of Maryland, College Park with a Mathematics/Computer Science major. Even with that difficult major, I took as many of the required difficult courses as possible at the beginning of my freshman year so I could complete them before losing my initiative.

One of the goals at that time in my life concerned my academic growth. I *always* wanted to be the *best* at whatever I would do. During the summer of 1987 I took the College Success Seminar to help me be ready to handle the college courses that fall. It was a day long course that helped my study skills, goal and schedule planning. That course helped to prepare me for all of the work that lay ahead.

I had been a Christian since the age of 10 when I asked the Lord to come into my heart and was baptized. We have been members of Trinity Assembly of God since 1979, where my family has always been active. My mom has taught Sunday School and served in the nursery and other ministries of the church. I had been active in my church youth group and Royal Rangers, a Christian boy scout group, where I had many friends and was a part of many activities. I received the Royal Rangers Gold Buffalo award and was one of four Rangers from our church to receive the prestigious Gold Medal of Achievement in 1986. I was the 29th Royal Ranger in the Potomac District to receive the GMA.

I achieved social growth in many ways. On Saturdays and during my school vacation, I worked for my brother-in-law, Mike Kogok, in his delicatessen, The Gourmet Express, located in Bethesda, Maryland. I was courteous and quick while I ran the cash register. Even on the busiest days I could keep up with the heavy flow of customers in a friendly engaging manner. During the week, I would help prepare catering orders, salads, sandwiches, and soups.

I was the only person working for Mike on Saturdays, so he allowed me to have complete control over the deli. In addition to performing the tasks necessary to running an efficient deli, I would make an attractive sign on a blackboard describing the food that we had available that day.

I also began to date. I escorted a girl to my senior year homecoming dance in 1986, the Valentine's Banquet at my church in February of 1987, and my senior prom in the Spring of 1987. My date for the Valentine's Banquet was named Christie. We went out as friends a few other times. One of the many tricks that she and two of her cousins played on me was to wrap my car with toilet paper and put a "For Sale" sign on it.

I've always had a sense of humor and enjoyed joking around with my friends. Little did I know that this sense of humor, as well as my determination, would see me through many rough times in the months that lay ahead of me.

The Accident

On Thursday, June 16, 1988, my brother-in-law Mike and I arose at 5:30 a.m. to go to work at the deli. After arriving at the store at 6:30 a.m., a typically busy June day began. While I greeted customers, rang the register and sliced meats, Mike produced the day's supply of pasta salad, gourmet desserts and specialty items. In addition to the normal flow of business that day, we produced a large catered lunch for a law firm located in Bethesda.

A friend of mine, Cannon Ferguson, the son of my pastor, William Ferguson, was also working in the restaurant that day. We all had a pretty normal day there. After the lunch rush was over, we ate lunch and cleaned up the store. Mike and I departed for home at approximately 3:45 p.m. and arrived home about 4:15 p.m. After arriving home, I decided to go to the bank to deposit part of my paycheck. I got my bank book, told my mom that I would be back in 15 minutes, and hurried out the door.

About ten minutes after I left, it began to rain *really* hard. My mother, Marcia, remembers hoping it would stop before I got home.

4

"When he wasn't home in about a half-hour, I became concerned, so I called two of Mike's friends to see if he had stopped by and had forgotten to call and say where he was. When neither friend had seen him, I began to pray."

Cannon and his family were preparing to have a cookout at their home around 5 p.m. A little later, a friend and member of our church appeared at the downstairs door of their house and told them that his wife had just driven by an accident scene and she was sure that the car involved was mine.

She was right. I had been involved in a tragic car accident. Witnesses told me later that it had happened like this:

On a four-lane road, a van was driving in the right lane heading west. I was in a small car travelling east in the right lane. The van swerved around to miss a car in front of him, crossed a double yellow line, and hit my two-door hatchback on the front left corner. It took the paramedics at least a half-hour to cut me out of the car. It had just rained, but the rain didn't play a significant factor. The eyewitnesses had no problem slowing down.

Recognizing that the car was mine, my friend stopped and asked the police if they knew who had been involved in the accident, but they couldn't tell her until my family was notified. They did tell her which hospital I was taken to, and a message was relayed to my pastor and his family. After telephoning other people and calling our church prayer chain, Cannon and Pastor Ferguson went immediately to Prince George's General Hospital in Cheverly, Maryland.

"Mortalizing" Realization

Nothing like this had ever happened to one of Cannon's close friends, so he remembers worrying and praying very hard.

"Seeing someone that you have known since the age of nine or ten in an awful situation like this at the mere age of 19 [my age at the time] is a terribly mortalizing realization," remembers Cannon. "Even though you hear of such accidents happening, it's not as real to you as when you know the person on a day-to-day basis. My heart went out to Mike's family."

My pastor, William Ferguson, remembers: "I had just come in from my daily duties when I learned that Mike had been in an accident, and that the car was pretty badly banged up. No one knew how badly Mike was injured. My immediate response was to try to call the house. I couldn't get anybody on the phone, so I drove over to the house. When nobody was there, I drove over to the accident site. I was told where it happened over in front of Frenchman's Creek Apartments on Riverdale Road, so I went over there and, of course, the police were still cleaning up the debris.

"The car was sitting along the edge of the road and I talked to the policeman who was directing traffic. I told him that the young man who was in this car was a member of the church that I pastor. He told me they had taken him to Prince George's General Hospital."

CHAPTER 2

Critical Care

When I first arrived at the hospital, it took the shock/trauma team about two hours to get me out of shock. They immediately operated to stop the bleeding inside. At that time I was being prepared for surgery and given computerized tomography (CT) scans to determine the extent of my injuries.

At approximately 6 p.m., a nurse from P.G. Hospital's shock/trauma unit telephoned my mom and told her that I had been in a serious car accident. She told her that I was in critical condition and to drive carefully to the hospital *immediately*.

"I didn't know what to think except 'Oh, no!,'" recalls my mom. "I called Michael's sister, Karen, and we prayed to leave him in Jesus' care to heal and comfort. That's all we could do. We left a note for my husband, Phil, and asked a neighbor to let Michael's brother-in-law know what had happened and where we were.

"Driving to the hospital, Karen and I did not know what to expect. We had no idea what kind of injuries he had received. We ached for him because we were sure he was experiencing some pain and discomfort.

"We found the nurse who called in the emergency

room. She ushered us into a small, private waiting room. She said we wouldn't be able to see Mike for a while because they were taking some CT scans, but she would have the doctor come out when he could. I asked if there were any police around who knew where the accident had occurred or what had actually happened. She said she'd find out, and soon she sent in one of the policemen who had arrived at the accident scene after Mike had been taken to the hospital. He was sent to reconstruct the accident."

As my family learned some of the details of the accident, they also discovered it was *not* my fault. Later, they learned from witnesses that it was an unavoidable occurrence. The Lord surely kept me in His hands.

When Pastor and Mrs. Ferguson got to the hospital they found my mom and sister, Karen, in the emergency waiting room.

"My first reaction was 'Lord, don't let him die,'" remembers Pastor Ferguson. "I could tell when I saw the car that the fact that Mike was still alive was nothing less than a miracle."

My mom recalls, "I really didn't want to call anyone until I knew something or had seen Michael. I remember thinking, 'Is this a nightmare or can this really have happened?' My mouth felt dry and I felt numb as we waited for my husband to arrive."

My surgeon, Dr. Casibang, met my family and told them about my condition. I was bleeding internally, my right arm and leg were broken, and more seriously, I had suffered severe head injury from the accident.

"The doctors did not give us any kind of prognosis at the time," remembers my sister Karen, "but I did some of my own, mentally, having been given a clear picture of Mike's present condition. The struggle between faith and reality is a tough one. Knowing for a fact that Mike was in condition "A" [meaning the only thing in his favor was that he was alive] and also believing that with God anything is possible, is a seesaw I rode on for most of the night. I really believe God won in my mind and heart, but doubt does not give up easily. That is when dark thoughts try to enter in."

After my dad came home from work and read the note telling him where my mom and sister were, he rushed to the hospital to find out how seriously I had been injured. He had an extremely difficult time dealing with the fact that I had been involved and injured in an accident. Not knowing and waiting made him feel *very* anxious, but having friends there helped out a lot.

Waiting and Praying

All during the long wait, people began to come to the hospital out of their concern for me and to be supportive to my family.

"It was comforting and touching to see them arriving and staying with us and to know how much they cared," my mom fondly remembers. "They waited with us until the doctor finally appeared to tell us what had been done and when we could see him. I remember some of our friends brought in drinks and sandwiches, but I had no appetite."

"We had prayer and then tried to encourage each other in the Lord," remembers Pastor Ferguson. "We knew that Mike was a Christian and that his family had been serving the Lord for many years. The fact that God had spared his life in the accident thus far gave us faith to believe that God had something far richer in store."

I was in surgery for approximately 3 hours and 15 minutes. The doctors placed an Intracranial Pressure (ICP)

Monitor, or bolt, in my head for the next two weeks so they could monitor pressure inside my head. I was put on a mechanical ventilator for two weeks. Afterwards, a tracheostomy was inserted. [A tracheostomy is a tube which goes from the exterior of the throat into the windpipe thus allowing for an adequate exchange of air.] Since I could not eat through my mouth I received liquid food in chemical form called hyperalimentation by IV. Later liquid formula was put directly into my stomach through a feeding tube. My accident was so serious that the only thing in my favor was the fact that I was still alive.

"We were given a further update during Mike's surgery," remembers Karen. "There seemed nothing to do but hear what the doctor said and receive it. Mike would not be ready for his family to see for some time yet. I don't believe my faith wavered too much now, because I rationalized that these doctors were not Christians and they were telling us what they saw in the flesh, making no allowances for God. I do remember my dad having a hard time and that seemed to increase my faith. I remember getting angry and telling him that if things were really that horrible after all, he could mourn and grieve for the rest of his life, if necessary, but until we knew otherwise, it was our duty to believe, pray and have faith. Such a lofty, noble statement! — so my faith was made stronger by the doubt and worry of others.

"Everyone handles their emotions differently, and in ignorance I found that my faith was stronger. I guess that is why we are supposed to have the faith of little children. With no intellectual sophistication, we can accept what we know God wants us to do and believe. Once we begin to rationalize and judge, our human frailty can destroy our faith. I suppose because going all those hours with nothing substantial or tangible to hold on to, with respect to Mike's

10

condition, it was fairly simple for me to trust. In fact, I think I was glad for the hours that we waited with no real news. The moment of trust would come soon enough when we were told we could see him."

Diagnosis: Severe Brain Stem Injury

By the time my surgery was completed, a dozen of my friends and my youth pastor were waiting with my family. Dr. Casibang came to meet them and told them the news: I had suffered *severe* brain stem injury. The prognosis was not good. My spleen had been removed to stop the bleeding. They had tried to set my arm and leg a bit and put a cast on each. The cast on my leg was open so that a wound on it could get air and heal. During surgery I had been given about six pints of blood, but I came through fine. While I was in the Recovery Room and before my family was able to see me, a bed was being made available for me in the Critical Care Unit. My family finally got to see me around 2 a.m., after an eight-hour wait.

My sister Karen remembers seeing me for the first time: "Mom, Dad, my husband Mike and I entered and stood around Mike's bed. He lay very still. Everything was quiet except for the artificial respirator that assisted his breathing. That in itself is an ugly picture if you have never seen one. He was pale from loss of blood and shock, and slightly swollen and bruised from his injuries. There were multiple cuts and abrasions and an open cast on his leg. The room, or maybe it was him, smelled to me like sickness and death. I also remember thinking that in his present physical state, he appeared to have aged. I can only guess that the shock to his system and the swollen appearance of his face seemed to enhance this perception,

11

but while I recognized him as my brother, of course, he was different from the young man who had left the house that afternoon. Then he appeared slight in figure, youthful and still boyishly young in face, but now his countenance reflected such a battered and worn look that it was as though he was almost a different person."

In God's Hands

When my dad was first able to see me, he thought I appeared to be *dead*! The doctors kept emphasizing that my diagnosis was *severe* brain stem injury. Even though my mom and dad kept hearing negative reports, they needed to ignore them, since they had placed me in the Lord's hands.

"I would not consider the gloomy predictions of the doctors and nurses, but testified of my faith when they spoke to me of Mike's future as they saw it," remembers my dad. "I prayed a lot and, with our church family, pleaded with God for a miracle and claimed it for Mike."

"That night, we really didn't comprehend the severity or extent of his injuries," recalls my mom. "The fact that he was still alive gave me hope. After seeing Mike, I felt relieved that his external injuries were not as bad as we thought they might be. He looked pretty much like himself except for some swelling. When we noticed how many machines he was hooked up to and how many needles and tubes were stuck into him, we realized he would probably not have survived the accident if he hadn't been taken to a shock trauma hospital as soon as he had been."

"We could not stay long," remembers Karen. "I think we probably touched him lightly and prayed as a family, and then each of us went home to our own personal grief. I think I cried mostly for Mike, for what he was going through, conscious or not. I grieved that he had to suffer and that his body had taken such a beating. I also cried for the fear of what his future might hold if the doctors *were* right.

"In bed, reflecting on the whole evening, fear was able to rush in where it had not been able to before. I still prayed and cried out to God, but thoughts kept interfering. I would be lying if I said that it never crossed my mind that perhaps Mike would have preferred to not have survived this accident — I was so grieved about his condition and suffering. But that thought was angrily dismissed as quickly as it came. I obviously would not have felt any better about his accident whether he lived or died. Incredible are the thoughts that can enter a worried mind uninvited. In any event, that thought has never revisited me.

"I did wonder how Mike would handle things if it turned out he did suffer permanent damage in one form or another. He had never been one to tolerate less than the best. While releasing my fear and sadness I also cried for Mom and Dad and what this meant to them. Obviously it never occurred to them that Mike would achieve adulthood only to be devastated in some manner by a tragic accident. I worried at their own fears, for how this would change their lives as well as Mike's."

"I slept very little, if at all," remembers my mom. "I remember experiencing a wave of heartache and then I would silently cry out, "Oh Jesus," and the heartache would be lifted. Then a littler later, I would feel another wave of aching and again would silently cry out to Jesus, and He would lift the heartache.

"The Critical Care nurses told us that we could call the hospital at 6 a.m. to hear how Mike was, but we could not see him again until noon for 15 minutes, and then not again until 6 p.m. Only one to two family members could see him at a time. When we called, they said there had been no change. As long as he was alive, I was encouraged."

Friends and Family — Strength in Unity

The following day, my mom began calling some of the relatives to let them know I had been involved in an accident. My Uncle Don and Aunt Geneva from Front Royal, Virginia, came over in the morning and spent the day with my family and visited me in the hospital. More visitors from our church came and had to wait in the waiting room because only family could see me.

My mom and dad, my sister Karen, and her husband Mike visited me during both of the visiting hours in Critical Care. My next-door neighbor let the neighbors know how I was doing.

My best friend, Tom Middleton, wanted to come see me as soon as I could have visitors. He and his family stopped by the house twice to ask about me.

"I had a great many memories running through my mind and all I wanted to do was to talk to Mike," remembers Tom. "My first thoughts were that if he died, I would be upset I didn't get to say goodbye. When I first saw everyone at the hospital, I had an empty feeling in my stomach, everyone's faces were white and starry eyed."

Some friends from church stopped by my house while my family was out. They left a card with a poem for me. So many people cared!

The next day the youth group at church devoted their entire service praying for me. "Our church youth group met and took a group picture," recalls Pastor

Ferguson. "Everyone signed it and brought it to Mike's room. A 24-hour prayer vigil began where volunteers would take one-hour segments around the clock. This continued until Mike showed visible signs of coming out of the coma. The people of Trinity Assembly of God were determined in their hearts to touch God for Mike."

Gloomy Predictions

"It was hard to concentrate on anything but Mike that day, wondering if he had awakened," recalls mom. "As we called our relatives and friends, we could only tell them that Mike had been in an accident and repeat what the doctor had told us. We didn't have any knowledge yet of what "severe brain stem injury" and "possible diffuse contusion in the cerebellum" meant.

"The day after Mike's accident, we were given some photocopied papers and a booklet explaining brain injuries and the different stages of recovery. We were to learn that the brain stem is located deep within the brain. Although it is small in size, it affects important functions such as the state of arousal, arm and leg movements, and eye movements. The brain stem provides the connection between the brain and spinal cord, controls levels of consciousness, and coordinates blood pressure, pulse and breathing. The brain stem is perhaps the most dangerous area of the brain to damage since it controls consciousness, alertness, and basic bodily functions, such as breathing and heart rate. The brain stem is the connection of the two hemispheres into the spinal cord and is where the 12 cranial nerves originate. Michael also had suffered widespread bruises in the cerebellum, the part of the brain that controls skilled muscular coordination.

"The nurse that gave us the written materials told

Karen to prepare herself and us: Mike would never recover and would have to live the rest of his life in a nursing home in a vegetative state. We felt news like that so soon after his accident was cruel and enough to make basket cases out of anyone who didn't believe in miracles. Also, we realized the hospital felt giving no hope was better than giving false hope or encouragement, but we *strongly* disagree.

"I will say that the doctor who performed Mike's surgery told us to be *hopeful*, even though he would later write in his medical records that he expected Mike to remain in a vegetative state. We appreciated his allowing the possibility for a miracle to occur."

According to the Maryland Head Injury Foundation, the most feared outcome after serious head injury is the vegetative state — a condition in which the individual opens his or her eyes but does not focus on anything, utters no intelligible sound, and makes no meaningful responses to any kind of stimulus. Sleep-wake cycles may be normal, and some food may even be swallowed reflexively. Many patients go through this state briefly when emerging from coma, but fortunately, only a very few — estimated at 3 percent — remain permanently in this condition. In the early days after injury, families are sometimes frightened by the possibility that their loved one will remain vegetative. There is no way to predict, but this outcome is rare.*

"The first week whenever we went to the hospital to see him during visiting hours, there was always a church brother or sister in the waiting room," remembers my mom. "They weren't allowed to see him, but their presence let us know how much they cared, how much they were praying, and how much they wanted to help. Gestures of love like that is what helped to sustain us in our grief."

Coping with Reality

Coming to terms with their own mortality during our carefree teenage years was one of the hardest things for my friends to cope with. Most of my friends have related to me that they felt confused and upset, not just for me and my family, but because for the first time in their lives, they had to come to grips with the reality and possibility of their own death.

"I remember seeing Mike for the first time one or two days after the accident," remembers my friend Cannon Ferguson. "I couldn't believe it when I saw him. If I didn't know for sure that it was him lying in the bed, I would have never believed it. He had so many apparatuses and tubes hooked up to him. The thing that really shocked me was the bolt that he had in his head to try to relieve the brain swelling. From that day I knew that nothing short of a miracle from God would be able to return him to perfect health or even consciousness."

My best friend, Tom Middleton, recalled: "My first feelings when I saw Mike were that of disbelief. I could not believe that something that bad could happen to such an innocent, great friend. Mike wouldn't hurt a fly and would always help you with something. The Mike that was before my eyes lying in that hospital bed wasn't the Mike I knew. His face and body were swollen and there were tubes and machines all around him. I was afraid that he was in a lot of pain. I knew Mike didn't like pain.

"Other thoughts after that day at the hospital hit me: That could have been *me* in the accident! That could have been *my* parents or other friends I had. Why did it have to happen to such a good guy? He would be a first close friend to die in a car accident. Mike wasn't drinking, he didn't do drugs, he was such a great guy. He had so much to offer the world.

"I knew Mike was a fighter, but this was a tough battle. I thought he wouldn't make it. It seemed that a miracle would have to happen to bring Mike back into this world."

Another one of my good friends, Tom Timmes, recalls: "The news shocked me. I had to think about why he had the accident. It was confusing and it upset me a lot. It made me think about my own mortality and how quickly things can happen. I was very concerned about his health and how his recovery would go.

"Mike was still deep in a coma the first time I saw him," remembers Tom. "One of his eyes was slightly open, but glazed and not focused on anything. His face was still swollen a bit and some cuts were still visible. The bar [bolt] used to monitor brain swelling was either still in or had just been removed. His head had been shaved in that spot, giving him a radical haircut. It was hard to see Mike like that because I wanted him to wake up and relieve everyone's tension. I, like everybody else, was praying for him. I wanted him to wake up and tell jokes again. I wasn't too sure what to say to him. I would say things, but also ask questions — questions he couldn't answer yet."

Drawing Strength & Comfort

My mother reminisces: "Our personal relationship with the Lord Jesus Christ, our faith in God, as well as all the prayers and expressions of love and concern from our immediate family, our church family, friends and neighbors, is what sustained all of us. I knew without any doubt that my strength, peace, and joy came from God.

"Daily reading of the Bible, spending time praising God, and praying for others have for many years been a source of strength and comfort. God has never failed to be there for me, even in times of sorrow and disappointment. I knew He would again sustain me and all of us if we would let Him.

"Even though we knew God *is* sovereign, we had placed Mike in His care and were believing Jesus to miraculously heal him, our hearts still ached and were heavy. We knew we needed to spend time together as a family and with some friends crying out to the Lord in our pain and praise Him for being with Mike and sparing his life.

"We needed to pray until we felt His peace. We left the hospital and headed for our church. The young people were in the sanctuary. We let them know that we would be in the chapel and they would be allowed to join us. Several of the youth did join us, as well as a few friends. As we praised the Lord for all He had done and what we believed He was going to do, we felt a peace come over us allowing us to sleep well that second night.

"We would be going through some deep water emotionally, for three months and three weeks, as we watched and waited for Mike to wake up and show some improvement. I remember reading in the Bible many verses for encouragement:

> *'When thou passeth through the waters, I will be with thee; and through the rivers, they shall not overflow thee; ... For I am the Lord Thy God...' Isaiah 43:2*
> *'Be strong and of good courage, be not afraid, for the Lord Thy God, he is that doth go with thee. He will not fail thee nor*

forsake thee.' Deuteronomy 31:6
'I sought the Lord and He heard me, and delivered me from all my fears.' Psalm 34:4
'Commit thy way unto the Lord; trust also in Him and He shall bring it to pass.' Psalm 37:5
'But they that wait upon the Lord shall renew their strength...' Isaiah 40:31

"I was also comforted by the fact that before Mike's accident, he had recommitted his life to Jesus Christ and wanted to live for Him," recounts my mom. "Each morning when he was home for breakfast, he and I used to listen to Christian music. Our favorite was the Scripture song with the verse 'Thy word is a lamp unto my feet and a light unto my path.'"

"All the time Mike was in Prince George's Hospital, I visited him almost every day," recalls Pastor Ferguson. "Of course, on a day-to-day basis there was not a lot of signs of progress. But after a period of time I did notice the swelling recede and he did look more like Michael. The scrapes and scabs healed slowly and he began to look his normal color again. But it was still many weeks before his eyes would open a little bit. There didn't seem to be any pupil dilation to show whether or not he was focusing on anything. Sometimes when we would talk, his eyes would seem to drift in the direction of the sound, but of course, he was still not able to let us know for sure that he was hearing anything."

My dad remembers: "Every day I expected him to improve — open his eyes, move, anything. That was all I thought of. I often questioned the nurses, probably bugging them to death, but I didn't care. Somehow I just didn't believe the prognosis they were giving."

Some of the things the nurses suggested my family do the first week after my accident were to make posters showing pictures of my family, home, yard, room, church and friends so that if I woke up, I might recognize something familiar. My church youth group made a poster, and different friends wrote letters and brought balloons.

"We also made tapes with us talking to Mike for him to listen to, in case he could hear us," recalls Marcia. "We brought in his favorite Christian tapes to listen to as well. We prayed for him each time we saw him and thanked God he was still alive. We claimed the Scriptures in the Bible for Mike that have to do with healing."

I received very crucial care in Prince George's General Hospital from June 16 through August 23, 1988. I was relocated to Bryn Mawr Rehabilitation Hospital (BMRH) in Malvern, PA., on August 23. All this time I knew nothing of this activity.

*Guidebook on Head Injury, by the Maryland Head Injury Foundation, p. 3, 1990.

CHAPTER 3

Bryn Mawr Rehabilitation Hospital

On August 23 my mom and dad arrived early at Bryn Mawr to take care of admissions and fill out the necessary insurance forms. One of the nurses wrote the message on the board that I would later wake up and read.

"I was relieved when he was well enough to go to Bryn Mawr," remembers my dad, "and that he would get the best care available. The care he got was very pleasing to me. I liked the people there a lot."

The Sunday after I arrived there, my nurse placed her finger over my trach to see if I could breathe through my mouth and nose. I did fine for the few minutes she kept her finger there.

That evening after suctioning me, my primary evening nurse went ahead and put the button over my trach to see how long I could breathe on my own, since my family told her about the earlier experiment. I did very well again except for a few hiccups and a cough, and she said that was *great*. When it was time for my family to leave, they were looking forward to knowing how much longer she kept the trach button on that evening.

My mom and dad were back on August 31. They

22

three hours before I had trouble breathing. That was good for a start. I had only tolerated it for about a second at Prince George's Hospital. They saw me in the morning to watch my therapy and would later talk with the team of doctors and therapists who worked with me to hear how they thought I should be progressing.

Things didn't look real good for me. Still comatose, I was basically a vegetable and had very little or no muscle control. My family was told I would need a skilled nursing facility after my predicted discharge date of November 1, 1988, unless I showed some improvement.

Physical Therapy

My parents returned that next Wednesday just as my physical therapy began in my hospital bedroom. Johanna was my first physical therapist. In the afternoon, my physical therapy was in a therapy room where my mom and dad helped. Completely supported by Johanna, I knelt, sat on, and then straddled a big oblong ball which faced a mirror. Johanna told my family that I needed to wake up before six months went by or I might be in a wheelchair for the rest of my life.

In a rehabilitation hospital, physical therapy goals are aimed toward functional independence. Initially, I was evaluated for a range of motion, strength, coordination, and functional ability. A treatment program was planned from this evaluation. Treatment included individual exercises to improve range of motion and strength and instruction and drilling in skills such as bed mobility and transfers. Prior to exercise, I could have received modalities such as heat, cold or whirlpool, but I didn't because it wasn't necessary.*

23

Signs of Alertness

Even though I was still in a coma, I showed a few signs of being alert. For example, when my brother-in-law Mike and my sister Karen visited me on a Saturday early in September, they said I opened my eyes and looked at them as if I recognized them when they called my name. It seemed like when I had my eyes shut, I would open them when my family called me by name, especially when they told me they had to go.

"When we visited Mike," recalls my mom, "we talked to him just as if he was hearing and understanding everything we said. We told him what we had been doing, what was going on at church, and who had called to ask about him. We read him the cards he had received. We read Scripture to him, prayed with him and played Christian music to him. We pushed him around in his wheelchair inside and outside. We held his hand and told him how much we loved him and how God was with him always when we couldn't be. When he would open his eyes, we would show him the cards he had received, pictures of us, his room, the yard, the church and some of his friends."

"Beating the Clock"

At this stage of recovery, I would be evaluated periodically to determine if a longer stay at BMRH would benefit me. These were called team conferences. My family was told that if my progress stopped, then I would be discharged and, chances were, would remain at or close to that state of recovery. If my progress continued to improve at a slow, steady pace, then my discharge date would be extended. This would be the indicator of improvement I made. Therefore, it was to my advantage to have as much time at BMRH as possible. Any delay in my discharge date meant I was making improvement. I was, in a sense, trying to 'beat the clock' in my recovery, trying to improve as much as possible in a short period of time.

Fortunately, team conferences were held every two weeks. I showed only minute improvement by September 14. Even though I was still comatose, I was getting some muscle control back, but nothing significant. My discharge date was still set for November 1, 1988. The next team conference was held on September 21. In that conference, they said I showed little bits of improvement and occasionally would follow commands and indicate "yes/no" on command. I showed enough improvement to have my discharge extended until December 1, 1988.

Anxiety

"We did live with anxiety at times," remembers my mom, "because of not knowing how to take care of Mike's nursing needs when the nurses weren't around. For example, changing the position he was resting in to another every two hours, making sure too much water didn't collect in his trach tube and cleaning him after he threw up. He was like a rag doll and couldn't move by himself or hold his head on the pillow. Unless his head was supported, it would hang over. He coughed frequently, and when he did, his head would move and need to be repositioned.

"There was one Wednesday night while Phil was at a prayer meeting that I remember sitting by Mike's head, holding his hand and crying as I thought of how the accident had changed his life and when he did wake up he would be afraid if he couldn't talk or move. I prayed that

25

he would be able to accept what had happened to him without being bitter. God has answered that prayer.

"In September when school began and I would see a University of Maryland shuttle bus, a wave of sadness would sometimes hit me as I would think of how utterly senseless Mike's accident was," recalls my mom. "I couldn't drive by the accident site for several months. I didn't look at the pictures the police took at the accident scene. Yet looking at them now clearly shows how God had spared his life.

"I didn't question God and ask 'Why?' but I did think at times what a waste, yet at the same time I recalled that God is sovereign and He had allowed the accident to happen for some reason."

A God of Miracles

Rev. Handel Price, a Pentecostal evangelist holding a three-day revival in October 1988 at my home church in Maryland, heard about my accident. After a meeting, he ministered in prayer with my dad on my behalf.

"I said to Mike's dad, you know, Mike might not be able to understand us in English," recounts Rev. Price, "but if we just speak in the Spirit there is a possibility that it will register." So Rev. Price drove to Bryn Mawr to pray for me twice that week, initially with Pastor Ferguson and my dad, then he came alone.

"And I believed that when we prayed and spoke in tongues at that time we were registering with God and registering with Mike," recalls Rev. Price. "And they said there was no hope! But now the hope was arising and I kept telling Mike's dad we've *got* to believe that Mike's going to walk and be made every bit whole. You see, I've been a fervent believer in God being a God of miracles. I never look at things as they are; I look at things as they should be and as they could be if we trust the Lord."

"We believed God gave Mike His peace while he was in the coma," remembers my mom. "All through his recovery we had seen the Lord going before us preparing places for us to stay while he was in Bryn Mawr for nine and one-half months. He led us to two nearby churches where our family was ministered to. Individuals of both churches came to visit and pray with Michael on days they thought the family couldn't be with him. Occasionally, we would be there and were glad to meet them. Their faithfulness to God's leading touched our hearts and Michael's life. The pastor of one of the churches let us stay in his home for as long as we needed."

One of those I came to know is Betty Jo Pollock from Bible Baptist Church in West Chester, PA. She used to come and visit me and read to me from the Bible when I was in a coma. "I always wanted to be encouraging," remembers Betty Jo. "After I read to Mike, I would say, 'I know you believe that, Michael.' Then after a couple of visits I found his Bible on the shelf and read from it. The verses that he had underlined were the ones I knew had special meaning for him."

* **Patient Information Booklet,** by Bryn Mawr Rehabilitation Hospital, PHYSICAL THERAPIST, p. 11, 1989

CHAPTER 4

Awake at Last!

When I awoke sometime after October 6, 1988, I vaguely remember seeing the sign welcoming me to Bryn Mawr Rehabilitation Hospital. There may have been nurses outside of my room, but other than that, there wasn't *anyone* around. I couldn't figure out where I was or what I was doing in a hospital. I couldn't dwell on those two questions because I was just too tired to care! I temporarily fell back asleep, but I was no longer in a coma.

It is part of the mythology surrounding coma that leads families to expect their loved one to awaken from this long sleep and return dramatically to normal within a few days. This rarely, if ever, happens. In fact, the process is excruciatingly slow and, at times, most distressing. The patient opens his eyes, but is totally unaware of the surroundings and may stare blankly, not focusing on activity around him. Gradually, he begins to focus, move a limb in a purposeful way and utter a word or two. Simple commands may be followed, but confusion is obvious.

This period may be accompanied by agitation or confusion, which is a reflection of the internal disorganization of the brain. This is often a frustrating

28

period for both patient and family. (Fortunately, this was one stage where the Lord intervened and I did not go through.) Later, as the brain heals, more organized and appropriate behaviors can be expected. All of this is part of the waking process, but technically, the patient is out of coma when the eyes open and meaningful responses are made.   [See Technical Chapter for levels of coma emergence.]*

During this coma emergence, I was transported in a wheelchair with shoulder straps, a head rest with a strap, and a lap board. I had shoulder straps and the head rest with a strap because my muscles that controlled my upper body were *very* weak. I was first given a shower on a shower table, and weighed by sliding my entire body off the bed onto a big, long tray. You can imagine how much it relaxed my body. I hadn't showered since the day of my accident.

I appeared to be awake on Saturday, October 8, when my mom and sister came in my hospital room. I followed them with my eyes and then my head as they moved around the room. They were overjoyed!

On October 10 while I was taking physical therapy, I showed my physical therapist Johanna the first sign I was awake. For the very first time ever, when she asked me to move my left thumb . . . I did! Then Johanna exclaimed, "Holy Moly! — he moved his thumb!" This was the very first time I had ever moved it when she asked me. Next she asked me to move my right thumb, which was a little harder. I didn't quite make it, but they could see I was trying.   That feat was the first sign for my physical therapist of my waking from the coma.

First Smile of Gratitude

I showed a little more progression on October 11. I moved my index finger for my Aunt Mary Jane and my mom. I did the same thing for my dad the following day. I believe that part of my gratitude for all of the love and care that I received was shown on October 16 when I smiled for the first time at my mom and dad. The primary day nurse in the Progressive Care Unit at BMRH wrote on my calendar that I smiled at her for the first time on October 26.

I had another record day on Wednesday, October 19 — I laughed out loud while they teased me with a battery-operated pig that my sister had bought me.

October 19 was also the date for a team conference. My discharge date at that time was still December 1, 1988. Even though I was awake, *all* of me wasn't quite with me yet. This may have been one of the reasons why the team conference concluded I was not able to cope with my disability. I guess then I never thought I was different.

Occupational Therapy

During my coma emergence, my occupational therapist's main objective was to retrain me to function optimally within my new limitations and to return to a productive lifestyle. This was accomplished through the use of facilitation techniques and through purposeful activities, like games, crafts, typing on a computer and baking cookies.

The occupational therapists worked specifically in many areas of my recovery. They promoted upper extremity function through achieving normalized range of motion, strength, and coordination in my arms and hands.

30

They were responsible for evaluating my ADL (activities of daily living) skills. This included dressing, grooming, household activities, bathroom mobility retraining and feeding during the latter part of my stay. It was my speech therapist who retrained me to swallow, move my tongue and close my mouth so no food would fall out.

The occupational therapy department's ultimate goal, through its treatment in simulated real life environment, is for me to achieve as much independence and personal pride as possible.*

Support & Encouragement

One thing I am extremely grateful for in my recovery is that I received **a lot** of support from my family and friends. Friends that either lived near the hospital or attended a nearby college were a great source of encouragement to me. Since my family couldn't always be there, my friends would take their place at times. I even received "get well" cards and letters from friends who couldn't be there.

On Halloween, a lot of the nurses and therapists wore ridiculous costumes. Christie, the girl I had dated in high school, lived near the hospital. She, her mother, aunt and two cousins brought me tiny pumpkins with faces drawn on them. These may seem like small kindnesses, but they were important to me.

On November 1, my motor abilities began to come back. In the morning, I surprised everyone by lifting my left arm when asked to — three times to my face. In the afternoon I surprised Johanna again by lifting my left leg up and I pushed down my right leg when she asked me to. My thumb and neck control were getting stronger.

Relearning Speech

Since I still couldn't communicate, I needed to find other ways to pass the time. It was then that I showed my love for games. I enjoyed playing Connect Four and, later, Monopoly. At a team meeting on November 2, my discharge date was postponed to January 5, 1989.

The following afternoon, Johanna put me on a tilt board for the first time. I really liked that. She only tilted the board up 20 degrees because even though I didn't feel dizzy, my blood pressure went up. That certainly was a good start toward standing up again.

Due to my injury, the Speech Department, also referred to as the Communication Disorders Department, initially concentrated on my cognition to see what I had remembered and forgotten. My first psychologist concentrated on that area as well. My first form of communication was blinking my eyes once for "yes" and twice for "no." When I had first awakened from the coma, my muscles were so weak that all I could do was to just move my eyes and head. I could not move my body at first.

My first speech therapist was also a graduate student. She helped me a great deal with my communication by creating an alphabet board with numbers and a few one-word commands on it.

Here is an example:

A	B	C	D	E	F	YES
G	H	I	J	K	L	NO
M	N	O	P	Q	R	I DON'T KNOW
S	T	U	V	W	X	NEW WORD
Y	Z					

1 2 3 4 5 6 7 8 9 10

Before my family went home on Sunday, November 6, they had all asked me questions and I was *finally* able to answer them using my new spelling board. First I would use my eyes to look at the letters I wanted them to write down. Later I would be physically strong enough to use my index finger to point to the letters that would spell the words I wanted to say. They all went home feeling good about how much I was improving and how great it was to have me be able to communicate!

More Progress

The next day, two of my Prince George's Hospital Critical Care nurses came to see me. They were really excited to see I was doing so well. They could see how God's miracle healing power was at work in my life.

I showed even more progress on November 10. On that day, my left arm showed more strength. Three therapists worked with me on trunk control, balance, and support. I performed well — showing more strength. I could bring and hold my neck up and turn it and hold it a lot better. I had very little muscle tone in my legs when Johanna had me bend them up and put them down. My right side was weaker than the left at that time. I could put my left hand on my right one and move it. My hand grip was much stronger that day.

In speech therapy, my therapist spent five minutes having me put my lips together and then open them, smile, and exhale, especially channeling it when I yawned. Johanna had me strengthen my stomach muscles and asked me to breath out and try to make sounds with my voice. I did a little on the 8th and 9th, but nothing on the 10th. She asked me questions like: "*Name three baseball teams; Name three football positions; Name three states and their capitals; and Name three shiny objects.*" My cognitive therapist had me listen for comprehension and then answer facts on a 6th-7th grade level.

While physical strengthening was a vital part of the rehabilitation program, recovery also involved attention to my emotional and cognitive needs. Cognitive retraining therapists at Bryn Mawr are certified teachers who provided remedial tasks to improve cognitive deficits.*

Pastor Ferguson drove up and visited me in the afternoon of November 11. I stretched out my left hand to shake and waved when he came in. He grabbed my right hand to shake and thought I had a strong grip. He later told my family that he knew why they were so happy! He sat in on my speech and cognitive rehabilitation therapies. Despite my lack of communication, the cognitive therapist told him I was testing cognitively at a grade 12 level and I was doing fine.

"At Bryn Mawr, which is about 150 miles from our church in Lanham, Maryland, I tried to get up at least once a month to visit," recalls Pastor Ferguson. "When I saw Mike daily I couldn't see that much change. But when there would be three or four weeks in between visits at Bryn Mawr, the change became more noted and more obvious. I remember the real victory when he was starting to be able to move his thumbs and blink his eyes "yes" or "no" when we asked questions."

My sister Karen was able to visit me during this time. We had some "good conversation" using the spelling board while she was there, although she tried not to wear me out with all of her questions. I tried to answer as many as possible, but I wasn't able to answer all of them.

Christie visited me at least once a week with other friends who lived nearby. It was nice to see familiar faces. Christie and her mother came to visit me around 6 p.m.

one evening. They wrote a message on my board that looked like this:

M	uch loved
I	mpossible to keep down
K	ing of Connect 4
E	ventually out of here!

When I showed them how I could raise and lower my bed, everyone warned me not to make a sandwich out of myself by pushing too many of the buttons together!

That Sunday, November 13, my brother-in-law Mike and I began to play Monopoly in my room at around 2 p.m. I rolled the dice until I got too tired. I was experiencing fatigue all to common to head injured patients. Fatigue came (and still comes) very quickly after the simplest tasks.

First Words: "Hi Mom"

I would continue to make what seem like little steps in my recovery, but in reality, they were big steps. For instance, on November 17, I spoke my first two words; they were "*hi*" and "*mom*". My mom and dad were filled with joy more than words could have expressed. They thanked the Lord for another milestone in my recovery. I struggled saying those words. I had to push the palm of my left hand down in order to obtain enough air pressure to speak. Near the middle of November my mom brought Thanksgiving decorations to my hospital room. The decorations made my hospital room seem more like a home away from home.

Before Thanksgiving my dad told me that if I would move my fingers or legs, he would do an imitation of the mechanical pig my sister had bought for me earlier. Little did he know I needed that kind of incentive! One day when my mom and dad entered the room, I wiggled my hands, kicked my feet, and laughed because I knew what my reward was going to be. My dad honored his word and imitated the pig. Oh, if I only had a video camera!

"Eating" Out

For Thanksgiving dinner I went to the downstairs cafeteria with my mom and dad, my sister Karen, and brother-in-law Mike. Since I was still receiving all nourishment through a gastric tube, I didn't get to actually eat with them, but I enjoyed the festive atmosphere. While there, my dad made a funny puppet by drawing a face between his thumb and forefinger. He gave it a hat by placing a napkin on top of his hand. We laughed hysterically as he made it talk and pretend to chew. People must have thought we were crazy!

Near the end of November, I was assigned a new physical therapist. She gave me a good workout, following in Johanna's footsteps. She had me standing with my hands resting on a table, then she had me bend each knee, one at a time. She also had me lift each arm up as high as I could. On a padded table she had me walk on my knees while she supported my upper body. And at that time, it was no easy job!

I had two more team conferences on November 30 and December 14, 1988. By December 14 I was able to maneuver myself in bed and give assistance in dressing — doing about 50 percent of the work myself. They said I still needed hands-on help with maneuvering and transferring in and out of the wheelchair. At that time, I needed hands-on help walking using a rolling walker.

Christmas — Home Away from Home

Before Christmas, the youth group from my home church visited me and brought me a sweatshirt they had all signed. The handbell and adult choirs from church performed at the hospital. They played and sang Christmas songs and came to my room afterwards.

"The church was really mobilized behind Mike and they felt it was a real outreach ministry to be able to take the cantata there," recalls Pastor Ferguson. "It was a real privilege to minister to Mike and the other patients and staff of Bryn Mawr."

Because of my improvements, the head rest and shoulder straps were removed from my wheelchair the week before Christmas. Close to the middle of December, my parents started to take me around the hospital grounds in our car. They did this to be sure that I wouldn't get sick from sitting on the inside of a moving vehicle. Thank God the motion didn't bother me, which is not always the case. I would also be using another wheelchair until my new one arrived. The wheelchair that I used was different from my original wheelchair — it could be folded up and put into a car. It was not as bulky or as big.

Because of this, I was able to celebrate Christmas 1988 off the hospital grounds and in my parent's hotel room, about 20 minutes away from the hospital. Celebrating the holiday with my family outside of the hospital was a real treat. It made that Christmas very special. Since I didn't know what to request, everything I received was a complete surprise. The Lord's miracle power at work in my body was the biggest Christmas gift I received that year. I also received many Christmas cards from relatives, friends, and acquaintances. For Christmas, Christie's mother made me a banner with "*Happy Birthday*

Jesus" written on it.

In a team conference on December 28, the hospital again extended my stay, this time until March 7, 1989 — my 20th birthday. I thought having them release me from the hospital would make a *wonderful* birthday present. I was still on a liquid diet received through a feeding tube in my stomach, but they anticipated I would have some control of swallowing and be receiving therapy for feeding as well. I was still using a wheelchair and my muscles weren't strong enough to maneuver it myself. Therefore, I would need hands-on help propelling it and cuing when transferring to and from the wheelchair by the discharge date.

* Taken from Maryland Head Injury Foundation Literature, 1990
* **Patient Information Booklet,** by Bryn Mawr Rehabilitation Hospital, OCCUPATIONAL THERAPIST, p. 10-11, 1989

* **Patient Information Booklet,** by Bryn Mawr Rehabilitation Hospital, PSYCHOLOGY & COGNITIVE RETRAINING SPECIALISTS, p. 11-12, 1989

CHAPTER 5

1989: A New Year, A New Life

As the new year of 1989 approached, I started a new therapy called aquatic therapy. Since I was unable to swim, my therapist would have me float on my back and try to help me walk in the water. That month I was also able to see two of my best friends, Tom Middleton and Tom Timmes.

"Mike was active and it gave me hope," recalls Tom Middleton, "although I felt like crying every time I left the hospital. Why does a person have to fight so hard to do the little things we take for granted now? Just opening his eyes was a great feat. Little battles were starting to be won and I started to think he was winning. I felt so bad for his family that they had to travel so far to spend time with him. Not only did Mike's life get upset, everyone around him was affected."

Eating Again

There were two more team conferences held in January 1989, and I was still showing gains. At that time, I was weaning myself off of the feeding tube and starting to eat. Since I had to relearn all eating skills, I had to start from the beginning once again — I would eat mainly pureed food and some with nectar consistency. I was still doing more than 50 percent of the work maneuvering myself in bed. I had also shown improvement in upper extremity strength and hand control, including some improvement in writing control with my right hand. My muscles did strengthen, allowing me to propel and transfer myself with help to and from the wheelchair. By that time, my discharge date had been extended to May 9, 1989. I was a little disappointed that I would be discharged later than my birthday, but I knew the extension was in my best interest.

February 22 was the last day I was given a night feeding through my feeding tube! I was put on a pureed diet or really soft food similar to baby food since I was unable to chew food. What a miracle! I couldn't taste all of the food yet, but it was so nice to eat with my mouth instead of having a nutritional liquid diet put directly into my stomach.

I began equestrian therapy, where once a week I would go horseback riding. Even though there were a few therapists who prevented me from falling off of the horse, that definitely was **not** one of my favorite therapies! I remember once I had to ride the horse *while lying down on my back!*

One day around my 20th birthday, Betty Jo Pollock, who came to read the Bible to me when I was comatose, came to visit me. She was from a nearby church. When she found out my birthday was coming up soon, she asked me what I wanted for my birthday. I answered in my newly found voice "MONNEE" with as much gusto as I could muster at the time.

Home for a Day!

On Sunday, March 5, 1989, two days before my birthday, I was able to go home for one day! The trip also included a visit to my church to attend the Sunday morning service for the first time since my accident.

My mom recalls that I recognized the area as we drove around the Capital Beltway in the Maryland suburbs. As I began to recognize familiar scenery, I began to say a few words: "Home, Home, Home."

We made a brief stop at my house first to borrow a pair of my dad's dress shoes for church. While at my house, I stopped by my bedroom because I wanted to see if I could recognize anything. It felt *so good* to be at home, even if it was only for one day.

When I pulled up in the car in front of the church, many people stood in the foyer to get a glimpse of me. As I was helped out of the car and into my wheelchair, the crowd parted. As I was wheeled into the church many people broke out into applause. The mood was very emotional. The youth group had tied balloons to my wheelchair. They also made me *"Happy Birthday"* and *"Welcome Home"* banners and signed one of them.

"When we announced that Mike was coming home for a day," recalls Pastor Ferguson, "there was a handclapping just like 'hip-hip hooray.' This was another real sign of progress in Mike's ongoing recovery. We felt that the hospital was confident he was making a good recovery or they would not run the risk of letting him ride in a car and spend the day at home. We felt like that was, again, another in a series of answers to prayer. The people flocked around to talk to him and encourage him. A cheer went up in the congregation that morning!"

After church, we drove home. My first meal at

home was baby food but, hey, it was real food. My brother-in-law Mike brought home an ice cream cake from the ice cream store where I used to work. I was able to taste that, and it was delicious! After I finished the meal I had a lot of visitors. It certainly felt great to be home, but I knew that for my own good it was just a day visit. I was really amazed by the number of visitors I had that afternoon. I had forgotten I had so many friends.

The following day, with the help of a nurse, I got to pull out the feeding tube from my stomach since I resumed eating! That was another giant step in my recovery. It was kind of disgusting because right before I pulled it out, I had just finished a chocolate shake. When I removed the tube, the shake began to spurt out of the hole in my stomach! Since I was still unable to chew, I was moved up to a soft mechanical food diet, which is both pureed and baby food that doesn't need to be chewed.

Around my birthday, March 5, Christie gave me a surprise birthday present — a roll of toilet paper. The following was inscribed:

> *To: Peakeman* (that is how she referred to me)
> *From: Chris, Mel & Jean*
> *(a.k.a. The 3 Musketeers)*

They probably wanted to see if I would remember that they used to wrap my car. I did.

Pizza!

There were two more team conferences held in March. The summary of the second one was positive, yet my discharge date was still set for May 9, 1989. I was showing continued improvement in mobility with bed activities and the wheelchair with limited independence. I was able to walk with moderate assistance about 60 feet with a rolling walker and doing greater than 50 percent of the work involved in bathing myself. When I began to eat, I promised myself that I would eat pizza before I was discharged. My mom took me to a nearby mall on April 16, and I ate pizza, not without some difficulty. I couldn't taste all of it but that was all right. My mom told me I wasn't missing much. Since I was able to chew a little, two days later they put me on a soft food diet which includes foods that are easy to chew, such as grilled cheese sandwiches and vanilla milkshakes.

More Evaluations

I had two team conferences in April and attended my last family conference on May 2. In that last team conference my therapists said that in physical therapy my strength was gradually improving. My right side was still weaker and my balance was starting to come, but it was delayed. I was fairly wheelchair mobile except for distance. I used my feet instead of my hands to move my chair. While walking I still needed stabilization in my right hip and needed to use a rolling walker.

In the Cognitive Retraining Program (CRP) at BMRH, I was at a high school level in reading comprehension. My rate of taking in facts was delayed, but the therapist said I could learn to work around that. I still needed to work on ideas for writing and structuring a sentence. However, I performed great in nonverbal reasoning.

I still had speech deficits. There were still some sounds I couldn't produce, delays in my swallowing, and my breath control was still decreased. I was also told that

I would *always* have speech deficits. It was really hard for my doctors and therapists to predict how much difficulty I would have in my speech. Motivation and inclination would enter into the overall outlook. Generally, they had seen gains and expected to see them continue.

My psychologist stated that I had an "atypical" response to accepting my injury. He thought this because I wasn't depressed about my condition. The reason I was not depressed is because I left my condition in the Lord's hands. Since he wasn't a Christian, he could not understand.

My other tests showed that I functioned like a generalized injury, and I knew what I was doing most of the time. It was concluded I might have less motivation and energy when I finally went home, but I had done a great job at coping with my injury. I needed a neuro-psychological exam in six months to better determine my I.Q. level. I was at Rancho level VII in my recovery. This is the second from the highest level called the Automatic-Appropriate level. I could complete common daily activities by myself, but needed to have someone with me.* (See Technical Chapter)

Another Miracle! Walking out of Bryn Mawr

My discharge date was still May 9, 1989. After over eight months of rehabilitation, I was quite relieved to hear I would be leaving within a week. I fulfilled another one of my personal goals on May 9 — to walk out of the hospital using my walker! Considering it was predicted that I would be a vegetable and then a wheelchair-bound patient for the rest of my life, I thought this was spectacular! What a miracle!

"Before Mike left Bryn Mawr we were told by one

of the critical care nurses that she felt his recovery would be a long one since he was in a coma so long," recalls my mom. "She said the hardest part of Mike's recovery after coming back home would be cognitive stimulation and lack of communication [being understood, as well as the fact that he won't be physically the same as before the accident] with his friends."

"She said young people find it difficult being around handicapped people their age as a rule. Isolation from friends makes family support even more important. If you have a speech impairment and physical limitations and can't get around without the help of others, life can become very lonely and frustrating. These would be problems Mike would have to experience and deal with until he recovers."

Looking back, I can see that these predictions came true to a certain extent, but with *patience,* persistence, skilled treatment and love from family and friends, I was able to keep fighting and "pressing on."

CHAPTER 6

Home at Last!

May 9, 1989 finally arrived! It was the day of my permanent departure from BMRH. When I arrived home, my mom made a delicious pizza casserole, and for dessert my brother-in-law Mike made a chocolate-chip-cookie pie at his deli.

"Mike's homecoming was a real high for me," remembers my father. "I was so happy to have him back where he really belonged."

All was not peaceful and calm when I first arrived home. Once, when transferring from my bed to the wheelchair, the wheelchair moved out from beneath me because the brakes were not locked. I did not hurt myself, but from then on, I checked my wheelchair brakes before I did any transfers!

"We were so happy to have Mike home but also a little concerned about whether we could meet all of his needs," recalls my mom. "He still needed a lot of help. He would not talk very clearly or fast and used a 4x6 card to point to the letter of the words he wanted to say. This took quite a bit of time. Mike could barely transfer into his wheelchair from the bed. He needed supervision when using his walker and sometimes hands-on support. Mike's voice was barely audible, so he needed to ring a bell to call us when he needed something. Because his bedroom was not completely wheelchair accessible he needed help reaching some things. As always, the Lord was our strength and gave us the wisdom and peace we needed to deal with all the stress we have experienced. Mike's sense of humor and dry wit have helped to keep us laughing through all the stress."

Therapy Resumes at GWRC

I only received three total days of rest from my rehabilitation. On May 12 my mom drove me to The Greater Washington Rehabilitation Center (GWRC) located in Silver Spring, Maryland, where I would be given speech, occupational, and physical therapy. Sometimes it took as much as one hour to commute to therapy, and I only received five days of vacation the whole year! It had to be continuous to work well. Mom was with me, devoting her time and energy every day.

My physical therapist, Michele, described me as a "very cooperative and well adjusted and patient" with my communication difficulties. She said I had "good rehabilitation potential as I received physical, occupational and speech therapy."

My physical therapist increased my strength and mobility and helped me to have coordination even though I had very little muscle tone. The jobs of my occupational therapists were to strengthen my upper extremity muscles and to eventually work with me on daily living skills. My speech therapist helped me mainly with clarity of speech and some cognitive exercises.

I had two occupational therapists and a speech therapist. Close to the middle of June 1989 when I was

47

unable to see Michele, the physical therapists who were able to see me attempted to walk with me in two different ways. I walked holding on to a railing with one hand and a therapist with the other hand. Two days later I tried walking with crutches attached to my arms. I didn't walk properly yet, but it was a beginning.

On July 21, 1989 I developed a high fever. I later found out that it was due to a middle ear infection. My mom was nervous because I had developed a fever of 102.4° at 4 p.m. She considered taking me to a hospital. Instead, my mom called our family physician. He wasn't familiar with the treatment of head injured patients. He called in an antibiotic to get my fever down, but he advised my mom to take me to the hospital if my fever didn't go down in an hour because he didn't know whether or not I would have any convulsions. My mom kept my fever down with cold washcloths and acetaminophen until the antibiotic was ready. My fever was down to 101° at 5 p.m., and back up to 101.2° at 6 p.m. It was finally back down to 98.6° at 9 p.m. Thankfully, because my fever had subsided, I did not have to go to the hospital.

The following day, my mom recorded my temperature as being 101.6° at 4 a.m. and 99° at 6 a.m. The whole episode really messed things up because I had planned to take a trip to the zoo with some friends. Now I was unable to go.

College Bound Again

I started college again on September 6, 1989. The therapists at GWRC supported me and surprised me with a delicious cake. I was on an extremely tight schedule. I was taking therapy all morning and then two non-credit classes in the afternoon. I managed to hold out on

48

September 6, 7, and 8, but had to quit on September 10 because it was tiring me out. I finally realized it was too much for me to handle so soon after the accident, so I withdrew from class. I believe it was then that I finally started to take notice of my handicap and that things weren't going to be the same. I also began transportation to and from therapy by means of Wheelchair Mobile Transport Service. This helped because it gave my mom more time to do things around the house.

Speech Milestones

Near the beginning of October I got a device that would help me with my speech. It is called a palatal lift and it was designed by Dr. Jack Light, a dentist and oral rehabilitationist. It is a removable device that fits into the upper portion of the mouth. It pushes against the upper palate so I can enunciate better and become more understandable to others.

Old Friends, New Experiences

My friend Tom Middleton took me to my former high school's homecoming game in October 1989. This time, however, I went to the game in my wheelchair. How many things I had taken for granted! Now, I really enjoyed being at an outdoor activity, the sounds and meeting with a few old acquaintances.

"When Mike moved home it was a great joy," remembers Tom. "I could finally start to see some of the old Mike coming out. His sense of humor was great. His outlook on recovery was great. I was really surprised he didn't get more angry at what happened to him. Mike has changed for life, and I have a hard time dealing with it sometimes. I don't think it was fair, but I think he has come a long way and is still going to go a lot farther. Mike is still recovering and it makes me happy to call him or see him and have him tell me he can get around the house without a wheelchair. I think his strong faith in God and the loyalty of his church friends have carried him out of that coma to where he is now.

"Mike is still my friend of yesterday and my friend of today, but he has changed from what I remember. But so have I. Sometimes I think of him as my little buddy. Mike grew taller and matured during his accident. The combination of these things make him different. But I still realize that he is the same great person inside. The things he does and his great sense of humor remind me of the days before the accident. Mike is a constant reminder to me to appreciate the small things in life all of us take for granted.

"I will always remember going and looking at the smashed up car and thinking 'how could someone live after such an accident?' I have learned that life is precious and can be taken away at any time. I have learned to enjoy myself and the smaller things in life. I am so glad that Mike is still around to enjoy the rest of his life.

"I have dreams of Mike running up the street again and asking me to go out and play around. His inner strength is an example to be followed. When I think I have something hard to do, I just think of how hard Mike had to fight for his life."

I thank the Lord that Tom has continued being my friend even after the accident. Most head-injured people do not keep pre-accident friends because of the awkwardness of the injury, loss of clear speech and inability to get around like before, but I thank the Lord He has enabled me to keep a few loyal friends.

"New" Life in Christ

On November 12, 1989 I rededicated my life to Christ. I didn't remember that before my accident I had a close relationship with the Creator, the Lord Jesus Christ. When I "woke up" from the coma, I had no memory of my previous commitment to Christ. I had forgotten what type of relationship I had with Him.

When I talk about having a relationship with the Lord, I mean more than just always being on my best behavior. Anyone can do that, but it isn't going to do you one bit of good unless you accept the fact that the Lord Jesus:

1)   left His seat at the right hand side of God (John 3:16),
2)   came to earth and was born of the Virgin Mary, (Isaiah 7:14), and
3)   died for all of our sins and conquered death by raising Himself from the dead (Romans 8:34).

You must also:

1)   realize that you are a sinner, along with everyone else (Romans 3:23),
2)   ask the Lord to forgive you for your sins (1 John 1:9), and
3)   ask Him to come into your heart and cleanse your mind and soul (Romans 10:9).

I still knew that God existed, but I feared Him instead of loving Him. This is an extremely important part of this story. I rediscovered that God isn't just a judge waiting for us to make mistakes. He is a forgiving God who will help each one of us live our lives in His footsteps through His

51

guidance. That can only be done by surrendering all of ourselves to Him. It is by my faith in Him that has continued to keep me going. His strength is there for me when my natural strength isn't.

I believe it was God who gave me the peace I felt when I awoke. It was God who also made me become understanding toward others and shielded me from any harm. I also know that the Lord continues to give me the strength to perform tasks.

While I was being taken care of at BMRH, my dad wrote a Scripture verse found in the New Testament of the Bible on the blackboard in my room. It is Philippians 4:13: "*I can do all things through Christ which strengtheneth me.*" That verse was not only encouraging, but true. My parents had found that verse taped to my desk at home and felt it must have been a favorite of mine before the accident.

Day Program Founded

In November 1989, another patient and I founded the Day Program at GWRC, directed by Peggy Meyerer, a speech therapist at GWRC. It was a long day of work from 9 a.m. until 4 p.m., Monday through Friday. The first hour was called the Gross Motor Group. It was a warm-up hour and a real workout. Next was accountability therapy for only a half-hour with Peggy. During that time, we planned our goals for the week and gave a current event. I then had Community Living Skills Group, on Monday and Wednesday. The budget, menus, and trips were planned during that hour-and-a-half session. Every Monday before lunch, the group would go to the grocery store. At first I used my wheelchair to go over, but within a few months I progressed to the walker with a basket attached to it.

The main occupational therapist did a lot of the nitty gritty work with the patients in the Day Program. She would allow us to handle the money delegated to us each week. She walked over to the store with us, allowed us to have some input in what we planned on eating that week, and was in charge of the group whenever we would go on trips. Since the other patient was Italian, occasionally we would prepare Italian meals, which I *thoroughly* enjoyed.

Before I started swimming therapy on Tuesday mornings, I'd have a Community Re-Entry Group on Tuesday and Thursday. On Thursday, we would usually take a trip for two hours. On Friday, I would have a Social Recreation Group. We usually created something, besides a mess, in that group. One of the things we made were holiday decorations. Then came my favorite time of the day — lunch.

When I went to the grocery store, I'd almost always buy enough food for the week. I'd need to either prepare my own meal or would help prepare the group meal. The only exception was when we would eat out on the trip on Thursday. Following lunchtime on Monday and Wednesday, I'd attend Pragmatics for half an hour. While in that group, we'd usually discuss how we would handle any problems we might encounter.

New Friends

Sally Mulholland, a friend I have come to know very well, was the business office administrator of GWRC, where I had rehabilitation. Since she was a real "character," we became quick friends. What made us "click" was the sense of humor we both shared — we both loved to laugh and make jokes. Because of this, we kidded around quite a bit. I first met her shortly after I started there, sometime before the day program started. Our first encounter led to my having informal computer lessons with her. When I say "informal," I mean that we ended up trading peanut butter cups for computer lessons!

One Monday, Sally remembers meeting me on the way back from the grocery store: "He was having a little trouble because he had so much to carry that it was falling off his lap in the wheelchair when he tried to wheel."

I told Sally I had bought too much stuff, so let's work out a trade — if she would push me in my wheelchair I would hold our groceries. So we hung some of the bags off the handles on the back of my wheelchair. I held the rest of it on my lap, and then Sally started pushing me back toward the Rehab Center.

Sally recalls: "Somewhere in there we started singing 'We're Off to See the Wizard, the Wonderful Wizard of Oz' — that lasted down to the barber shop, and then we somehow got into an extremely violent argument over the names of the seven dwarfs and we couldn't remember all seven. We could only remember six. When we got back to the Rehab Center, we decided we would, of course, go see Claudia, who would immediately know the name of the seventh dwarf, and she did."

I was getting so good using my wheelchair that I enjoyed chasing Sally down the hallways in the Rehab Center (and I usually caught her!).

"As soon as I got into the hall, it seemed I was fair game!" recalls Sally. "I had to look both ways because the fastest Mike ever moved was when he thought he could run me down with his stupid chair! And I remember one time when Mike caught me out in the lobby and there was a huge sofa...I was about to go home and he had cornered me against that sofa — it went around three sides of that

54

room.

"I walked up on the sofa, yelling for the receptionist to dial 911, that I was being attacked! I finally jumped off the other end of that long sofa and said 'Bye! I'm out of here.' Then Mike got to the point where he could maneuver so well he could get into the business office, and my office was off of that. One day, to my horror, I turned around and there he was blocking the doorway to my office saying 'Ah ha! You can't get out!' After that first time he blocked me in my room, my staff got wise and would warn me from then on with 'Head's up — he's coming.'"

Since then Sally and I still continue to keep in touch. She still helps me with my computer and our families have drawn close because of my injury.

More Therapy

Tuesday and Thursday were the days I would have Computer Cognitive Retraining with Peggy Meyerer. For half an hour, I'd either work on the group computer or make plans for a simulated trip.

On Fridays, I'd have physical therapy after lunch for one hour. Then I would have Adjustment to Disability. With a neuropsychologist, we would discuss any problems encountered during the week. Monday through Thursday, I went to physical therapy after the pragmatics or cognitive retraining groups. On Tuesday and Thursday, I would end the day with speech therapy. I'd finish with vocational time on the computer with Sally on Monday and Wednesday.

Driving Again — A Temporary Thrill!

During my occupational therapy in December 1989 I did something very exciting — I drove! Of course I had to have a driving instructor in the car with me. It felt great to get behind the wheel of a car again. My occupational therapist wanted to see what my driving capabilities were. My doctor felt that I had adequate cognitive skills for driving. I took a road test and tested "average to above average" on driving skills. I could then take the required reaction time test as well as the written and road test to renew my license. I was too busy with therapy to seriously consider driving then, so it was just a temporary thrill. Today I only use my license for identification purposes.

CHAPTER 7

1990: No More Wheelchair!

In January 1990, I began using my walker at therapy. When my parents found this out, they began to make me use it at home as well. Naturally, I was not happy at first because I had a fear of falling, but if they had not insisted, I don't know if I would have continued to progress. Trying not to rely on my wheelchair, I used my walker to go almost everywhere. Eventually, my ambition was either to use a cane or to do without any assistive devices at all. I would still use my wheelchair at times. Even though I was continuing to progress, I would still tire out.

Beginning in January I had an occupational therapy session twice a week to help re-strengthen my right arm, since it was still weak.

All I Want For Christmas ... Is To Walk

The staff of GWRC gave me a birthday party on March 7, 1990, my 21st birthday. It was a small celebration by the staff and therapists, but I appreciated it. One birthday present that I gave (and received) was the ability to walk around the 150 ft. track with my walker for

Sally's birthday, which occurs in the same month as mine. She had asked me to walk around the track four times for her fortieth birthday.

"Mike and I had lunch together one day before Thanksgiving last year," recalls Sally, "and we got to talking about Christmas. We also ended up singing silly songs like 'All I Want for Christmas is My Two Front Teeth,' and then I said, 'now seriously, what do you want for Christmas?' And Mike said, 'I want to walk.' I told him I didn't think he would make it by Christmas, but how about my birthday, March 1? 'I'll bet you could go around the track, couldn't you?'

"I told him I wished he could go around the track once for every decade of my life, because I was going to be forty. Mike got so tickled with the idea that he said, 'Nah, you're going to be sixty. I'm going to have to run around that track six times.' I said 'I think you can do it. You can get around the track four times. I don't care how, but you're going to walk, whether or not you have to use an assistive device.'

"Well, at the time we talked about it, it seemed like an absolute impossibility. But everybody had found out about it — that on my birthday he was going to have to walk around the track the number of decades I was. He did it! He had to use the walker, but he *did* get around the track four times." [She's lucky I got tired or I would have walked around it at least one more time! -MP]

Anger

It was around Sally's birthday that I got irritated at one of the other patients in the Day Program. We were in the kitchen when I heard her complain about her mental injuries. That ticked me off a little. To the best of my ability I told her, "Look, at least you can walk and talk! If anyone should be angry, it should be me!" Thank God that my anger didn't control me. At least I wouldn't allow it to. I have gotten angry but I control my anger by lifting it up to the Lord. What I mean by that is not dwelling on what I'm not able to do but thanking the Lord for even the smallest thing I can do. It was a very difficult thing to do at first, but it became easier to do as time went on.

Gardening

In April I visited Dr. Panagos, my physical medicine doctor who specializes in rehabilitation. He did not try to make any predictions for me. He just told me people may tell me that I will be unable to do things, but I won't really know until I try.

In May, I went into my backyard with my walker, got down on my knees, mixed the dirt up, and planted nine strawberry plants! I had never done anything like that since my accident. It took a little less effort to walk on the grass since I knew it would be a softer surface in case I fell.

Starting June 4, 1990 until the end of July, I dropped speech therapy altogether, and resumed vocational time with Sally on both Monday and Thursday. I was designated to have free time on Tuesday, Wednesday, and Friday. It was still a long day, but the time seemed to pass by quickly as the therapists continued to keep me busy.

"Excellent Progress"

June 16, 1990 marked the second anniversary of my accident. I remembered the date but not the event. A reality came to my mind: I've come a long way. I also saw my original neurosurgeon. He told me I was a

59

miracle. Now I even have the doctors telling me that my recovery is miraculous!

Considering the length of my coma and the extent of my injuries, my physical medicine doctor has rated my progress as "Excellent," and has said he has seen "very steady, gradual improvement in concentration, speech, coordination and strength."

My current physical therapist has seen improvement in my balance and strength, and has seen overall improvement with mobility.

They both agree that my optimism, faith, positive attitude and great family support have all been invaluable in my recovery process.

In July 1990, I had the *"privilege"* of experiencing my first memorable pain. When I was walking with my walker, I lost my balance and fell backwards with my tailbone hitting the hardwood floor! I didn't break any bones, but my rear-end sure hurt!

We took a pleasant trip that month in the Day Program to the Hard Rock Cafe and ordered chili. The reason the trip was so pleasant is because the chili was so delicious. My occupational therapist told me that she had never seen me eat so fast. Without realizing it until afterwards, I even had "woofed down" someone else's order! Considering that I was a fairly slow eater, that must have been some good chili!

Finally, at the end of July, I graduated from the Day Program. I would still, however, come three days a week for speech, occupational, and physical therapy.

CHAPTER 8

The "Famous" Michael Peake

In the early part of August 1990 my Aunt Helen and Uncle Larry from Washington state visited me. During their brief stay I bought an exercise bicycle. Even though I went to therapy three days a week, I was still able to get a nice workout every day at home on my bike.

I finished my occupational and speech therapy in September. Beginning in October, I would only be scheduled for physical therapy with a new therapist for three days a week. I also stopped using the wheelchair transport service. Instead, my mom drove me.

Court Dates: Trial & Guardianship Hearings

The trial for my accident was supposed to be for one week in September. Even before the trial, I had an inner feeling that everything was going to be all right. From that moment on I left it in the Lord's hands, and I am so happy that I did. Before the first witness was called, the case had been settled in my favor! I left the trial shaking the judge's hand and having him wish me the best for my future.

On October 2, 1990 I met with Dr. Panagos and

asked his opinion about my parents relinquishing their guardianship over me. My parents thought it was no longer necessary because I had regained enough cognitively to manage my own affairs, and my doctor agreed. On October 12 I met with my originally appointed court attorney. The last time she had seen me I was in a coma. She was really amazed; she said she had never had a *miracle case* before.

On October 26, the courts agreed I no longer needed a legal guardian. It took a month for the paperwork to get through but, once again, I left the hearing shaking the judge's hand and him wishing me the best for my future. Now that is rare! My parents were happy to relinquish guardianship. It meant less paperwork for them and would make my life more meaningful by handling my own affairs.

Another Car Accident!

On October 13, 1990, my mom, Sally and I were involved in another car accident. God miraculously intervened to spare us from injury, although we were shaken up. Because of God's protective hand, I felt no pain when my walker struck the temple of my head during the collision, and it didn't even leave a bruise! Some paramedics were in the area, the police were there within minutes, and so were the tow trucks. Sally joked that she was getting tired of having my guardian angel coming to my rescue!

"Small" Accomplishments

On Monday, October 22, 1990, I got to carve into a pumpkin that my dad bought. I carved a small "smiley" face on a medium-sized pumpkin. Then I cut out big ears from paper and added them on Tuesday. On Wednesday I finished it off with a bow tie and a top hat. I do believe it was the best-dressed pumpkin in the neighborhood!

On Thursday, November 1, I made my first attempts to walk in and out of therapy with my quadcane and a little help from my mom. [A quadcane is a 4-pronged cane. It is the next step forward in a handicapped individual's progression, after the walker.] The following day, I managed to walk in and out of therapy with my quadcane and *without help from anyone.* It was still a little soon to begin using a quadcane entirely, so I held off until a later date.

I was beginning to do small jobs around the house. I helped my mom trim some hyacinths and I cleaned out our silverware drawer. It may not seem that important, but it felt good to be able to accomplish those tasks.

On November 30, I walked around a department store with a shopping cart! No, I wasn't pushed by the cart, I was pushing it! I walked around the entire store. That wasn't a small distance because it was **not** a small store. This was another pleasure I had always taken for granted.

The Most Important Things in Life

Toward the middle of December 1990 I ate lunch with my lawyer, John Marshall, and his 4-year-old daughter. It was on that day that she finally was able to meet "the famous Michael Peake."

"I think one of the things that affected me most was to be able to watch a family, who has had a terrible thing happen to them through no fault of it's own, go through this ordeal," said John. "They were not depressed over it, but fought back, worked hard, and tried to recover as best they could. It taught anyone who came near the Peakes what courage, faith and strength, especially family strength, are really all about. It was proof to me that those things work — and those are really the most important things in life."

On December 16, 1990, our church choir performed a superb Christmas cantata. Before the cantata began, I felt something in the air, and it was telling me that **God was not finished with me yet.** I didn't know, however, how soon the next miracle would occur or what it would be.

Another Miracle: To Walk With A Cane

The following day, Monday, December 17, I was able to use my 4-prong cane almost all day — from when I got up and took my shower until that evening! That Wednesday, I used my 4-prong cane to walk in and out of my barber shop and church that evening. Then on December 20, I began to try taking a shower standing up. I still would use my shower chair for a little bit, but it was only temporarily there. I also used the grab bars installed when my bathroom was built.

I celebrated Christmas 1990 at my house with my parents, my sister Karen and brother-in-law Mike, and their baby, Rebekah. God gave me and my family a wonderful present that Christmas: *He enabled me to walk, unassisted, for a longer amount of time with my 4-prong cane.*

On Thursday, December 27, I was able to walk about 150 feet around a track at therapy with just a single-point cane, the next step forward in my progression. My therapist did have to help me twice, but it was a sign I was still improving.

My friend Tom Timmes came over from Virginia and stayed over New Year's Eve. I usually would tire out at around 9 or 10 p.m., but I ended up staying awake and playing Monopoly until 12:30 a.m. New Year's Day! When I finally saw the time, I couldn't believe I had stayed up that late. I started the new year off on the right foot (or feet) by having my mom remove the shower chair on New Year's eve. I was still using the grab bar, but still *without the shower chair.*

Taking a shower without the "chair" was another milestone for me because, for me, it meant I was a little less dependent on something else for assistance.

MIKE'S JOURNEY — A PICTORIAL REVIEW

The scene of the accident.

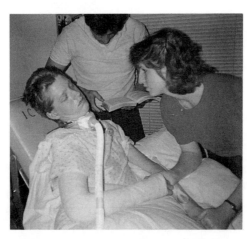

Mike's sister, Karen Kogok, and brother-in-law Mike Kogok, visit Mike at Prince George's General Hospital.

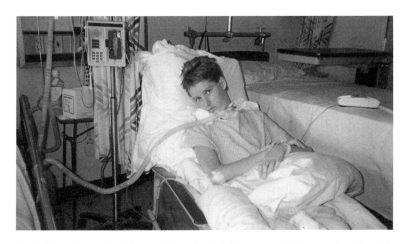

At Prince George's General Hospital, Mike opens his eyes, but is still in a coma.

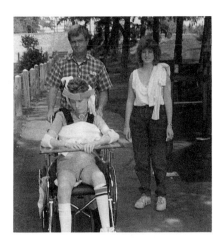

At Bryn Mawr Rehabilitation Hospital in Malvern, PA, his first weekend. Mike's father and sister Karen take Mike for a stroll around the lake beside the hospital. Mike was still comatose.

Even though Mike was still in a coma, physical therapist Johanna
Spagenberg works with him three months after the accident.

Mike, still comatose, appears to stare at you right in the eye.

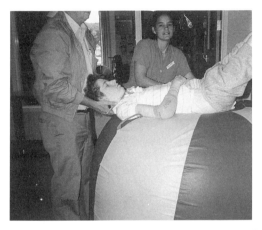

Physical Therapist Johanna Spangenberg with assistance from Mike's dad, continue to work with Mike while in a coma, this time on a big ball.

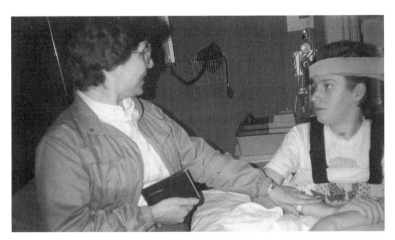

Finally awake, Betty Jo Pollock, a nearby church member, gives Mike some spiritual support.

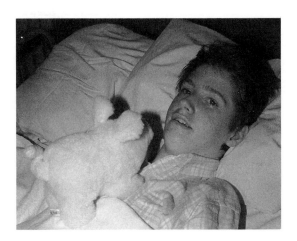

Mike and "Piggie." November 1988.

Mike's Dad, Phil, making a puppet at the Thanksgiving table in the hospital cafeteria. November 1988.

Mike and physical therapist Johanna Spangenberg look like they are "dancing" together during physical therapy.

Since he couldn't speak yet, Mike communicated by using a message board.

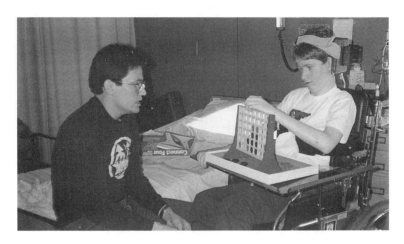

Mike and brother-in-law Mike Kogok play Connect Four.

The whole family gathers for a snapshot: (l to r) Marcia Peake, Mike Kogok, Karen Kogok, Phil Peake with Mike.

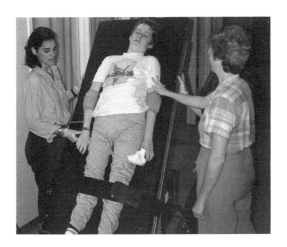

Learning how to stand again. December 1988

Mike is finally allowed to make a trip around a nearby mall with his mother. January 1989

Mike and his mom on the grounds of Bryn Mawr. April 1989

Mike eating pizza for the first time since his accident. April 15, 1989

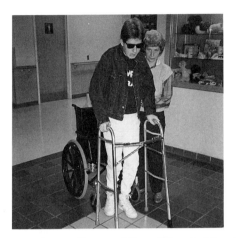

Mike fulfills his goal to walk out of Bryn Mawr! May 9, 1989

Home at last!

The "BMRH Grad."

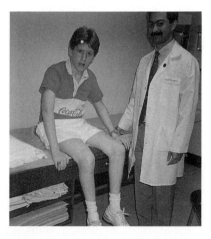

Mike's first visit to Holy Cross Hospital to meet with Dr. Andrew
Panagos, his Physical Medicine doctor. May 25, 1989

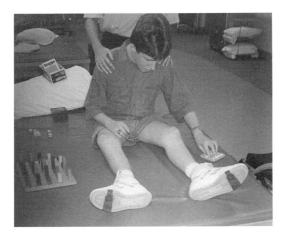

Mike continues therapy at Greater Washington Rehabilitation Hospital.

Lunch Break at GWRC's Day Program.

Mike planting strawberry plants in his backyard. June 1990

Mike graduates from GWRC Day Program. July 1990

Mike Peake in April 1993.

CHAPTER 9

1991: Setbacks & Miracles

Starting January 4, 1991, I began having problems with my sight, mostly in the morning. I wasn't able to focus on an object because the pupils in my eyes would rapidly jerk from side to side. Thankfully, I didn't feel any pain, had no convulsions and wasn't dizzy. The following day I experienced the problem nearly all day. That afternoon my physical therapist told me that my problem is known as "*nystagmus*" and recommended that I temporarily use my walker. Nystagmus is involuntary and repetitive rolling or jerking of the eyes. It is one of the results of a brain dysfunction. That Sunday, I did feel relief and I used my walker all day. However, I didn't resume using my shower chair.

On Monday, January 7, I went to a neuro-ophthalmologist in the morning. His assistant was amazed that I was not on any medication after my mom told her the extent of my injury. The neuro-ophthalmologist told me I had "jerky nystagmus to the right." I was scheduled for a magnetic resonance imaging (MRI) scan the following day at the Wheaton Imaging Center. An MRI scan is similar to a CT scan and can be used to find out what is causing nystagmus. The doctor was unable to tell without the test results. The test results would not come in for a few days so I had to wait. Having the MRI done was not as bad as I had expected. It was nice because I felt no pain and I didn't become dizzy. The last time I had an MRI was when I was coming out of my coma at BMRH.

The Lord has been and still is on my side. I could have felt depressed because, although I had come so far in my recovery, I still had to overcome this additional problem. Even today, I **know** that He is not finished with me yet.

Thursday, two days after the MRI scan was taken, my nystagmus bothered me only in the morning. On Friday I began to resume using my 4-prong cane for most of the day.

My physical therapist had transferred to Greater Laurel-Beltsville Hospital in Laurel, Maryland. I was discharged from The Greater Washington Rehab Center in Silver Spring, Maryland and continued physical therapy at Greater Laurel-Beltsville Hospital so she could continue treating me.

The results of the MRI scan were explained to me by my physical medicine doctor on January 17, 1991. I was relieved to hear that it was nothing serious. In fact, it was a good sign that my nystagmus began bothering me just in the morning. The results showed that I had some shrinking of the cerebellum and brain stem, but because my brain could still circulate the fluid within it, I was in no real danger. This is something that I will just have to live with.

A Few Small Steps Unassisted

On January 19, I took a few steps in the kitchen without *any* assistance. The Lord really made my day when He enabled me to do that!

The next day, my friend Sally came over and put more programs on my computer and set up my printer. I am so grateful, so pleased, to be able to use the computer for record keeping, typing correspondence and this book manuscript, and to play a few games.

On Tuesday, January 22, 1991, I once again began taking physical therapy at The Greater Laurel-Beltsville Hospital for five days a week. On January 25, 1991, I completely stopped using my walker to get around the house.

Fear of Falling

Another miracle occurred very early in the morning on February 2. A little after 12:00 a.m., I began taking a trip toward the bathroom with my quadcane. I began to lose my balance, but thankfully I didn't fall and managed to steady myself on my quadcane. I could have fallen onto the hardwood floor but, praise God, I didn't!

Many times I had asked the Lord to speak to me. During an evening service on Wednesday, February 6, 1991, the Lord did speak to me through someone else, inspired by the Holy Ghost. Someone prophesied, and the prophesy was for me. He said that I was afraid of falling and that I should not be afraid because He had His angels guarding over me. He was still healing me. With that assurance, I began to use my single-point cane as well as the 4-prong cane the following day.

CHAPTER 10

Sally's Miracles

I have been pleased to see Christ's influence on my family and friends. Without my even knowing it, the miracles I experienced in my recovery were inspiring other people as well. Beyond that, I was blessed to see God performing miracles in the lives of people around me and to witness the power of prayer.

On February 19, 1991, my friend Sally Mulholland called my mom and me to ask us to pray for her parents. Her mom was scheduled to have surgery for cancer and her dad had Alzheimer's disease. She said she knew that prayer would have a great influence because my miraculous recovery showed her that *prayer does work.*

Birthday Surprises & Special Gifts

About two weeks later, I celebrated my 22nd birthday in the beginning of March with my family. My brother-in-law Mike made a delicious meal of boiled, spiced shrimp. My sister Karen added to the enjoyment by making some scrumptious crab cakes. The two finished the meal off with an ice cream cake from the ice cream store where I used to work. The cake was a "tasty" surprise.

My physical therapist surprised me with a chocolate-almond cake. I was quite surprised that she would make a cake for my birthday, and I *forced myself* to enjoy it. It was great!

My parents and I ate dinner that evening at a seafood restaurant. When our waitress found out that it was my birthday, she and a few other waiters and waitresses sang me a *"Happy Birthday"* tune with a little twist.

I may not have expected too much for my birthday that year, but I certainly received a lot anyway. Through God's miracle-working power on my life, I have come a long way since my birthday last year!

Sally called me on my birthday and made my day with some exciting news about her parents: One of her sisters visited about four nursing homes, searching for one to place her father in. She really liked the fourth home. Miraculously, it was either owned or sponsored by a man that her father used to work for. When that man found that her father needed a nursing home, he made arrangements and enabled her father to get a room. In fact, a new 10-unit home had *just opened*. Since her father wanted to live independently and they had no rooms available in the other home, he would be the first one to live in the new facility in a room by himself, which is what he wanted originally!

The same day that Sally's mother went into the hospital, her father fell and hit his head and had to have stitches. While the doctors were putting the stitches in his head, they also found blood clots. They were able to remove them in time because the clots had been detected early enough. If he hadn't needed the stitches, then they would not have been able to detect the blood clots until it was too late. Another miracle!

Sally's family knew that her brother's brother-in-law

was dying, and he was only 33. Sally's brother had just finished a job and, as a result, was going to have some time off. A day or two after the brother stopped working, the brother-in-law took a turn for the worse. Because her brother's job finished at the right time, he was able to stay at home with the brother-in-law so he could die in peace. This was a very special miracle.

During Sally's mother's operation and much to the doctor's surprise, they were able to remove *all* of the cancer because it had not spread to the other organs. My mom and I were praying that no cancer would be found. The Lord Jesus didn't answer our prayers the way that we might have wanted, but He still answered them. Sally also asked me and my mother to write to her mother because she was really pleased when she found out that we had included her on our church's prayer chain.

On March 14, 1991 Sally called with some news about her parents. Her mother was doing fine, but her father began suffering from a subdural hematoma, or bleeding in the brain, again. Thanks be to God that he didn't feel any pain, but after it started on the 12th, he went into a coma the next day.

Sally called us when she returned from visiting her parents in Oklahoma. Even though her father was in and out of a coma, she reported some good news. The family found out the nursing home that her father was going into was not to be completed until about one month later. Since her father was in the hospital and unable to stay in the home, the parents would be able to save money on one month's rent and he would still be able to move directly into the nursing home they wanted. Also, Sally told us her mother appreciated the letter that we sent her and our continual prayers for the family.

During this ordeal, I saw an example of how God is

85

using my head injury to help others. On a previous date, I had shared with Sally that I didn't remember feeling any pain while I was in a coma. She shared that information with her mother and her sisters. They were comforted because their greatest fear was that he would remember the pain.

My mom and I told Sally we would be praying that the Lord would give the whole family a spirit of peace. God gave Sally an opportunity to comfort someone else while she was on an elevator in the hospital. Two ladies got on and they were quite upset, as if they received some bad news. One of them said to the other, "*I don't know what to pray for.*" Without hesitation Sally told them, "*Pray for peace.*"

Before her dad went into the hospital, God performed another miracle. A nurse had been taking care of him at his house. One day, she was downstairs while Sally's dad was supposedly sleeping. Without her knowing it, he got out of bed and fell, hitting his head on a table. A short time later, the family dog found him on the floor unconscious. The dog then went downstairs and barked at the nurse and directed her upstairs. He raised such a commotion that she went upstairs to see what the problem was. When she got there, she found the father on the floor. This was a very unique and out of character thing for the dog to do.

Testimony: An opportunity, not a tragedy

"I've always admired Mike's attitude," confides Sally. "Whether it's because of his personality or his faith in God, from the beginning he always had this very positive attitude. I would compliment him that he was able to do something, whether it was in his regular physical or

86

occupational therapy, or if he was able to do something on the computer, he'd say, 'Don't compliment me, compliment God.' And it was always amazing.

"It was interesting because when I saw Mike deal with his accident, he took it as an opportunity instead of a tragedy. He taught me a very valuable lesson: Your attitude makes a difference. He could have taken what had happened to him as a terrible tragedy and crawled into bed and stayed there for the rest of his life, and I don't think anybody would have really questioned it.

"Instead I remember him making jokes about being head injured. Mike would tell me he was H.I., and I'd say in his case that means humor-injured, and we'd both crack up.

"I remember very strongly seeing how he had taken something that, to most people, would be a tragedy in such dimensions that they would never be happy again. Somehow he managed to take it in stride. I remember going out to lunch one day with his mother sometime during the summer of 1990. I looked at her and said: 'It's surprising, you know, but I think Michael is happy.' And she kind of looked at me for a minute and said, 'You know, I think you're right.'"

As I have stated before, I have gone through periods of depression, which is common in head injury survivors, but mine have always been very short periods. The Lord *has* been good to me. That's what I think, and begin to be thankful. If I always dwelled on my situation, then I would not have come as far as I have today, and I won't continue to progress in the future. But I have progressed, and when I have a negative attitude, my progression either slows down or just dwindles.

"I remember Mike and I talking about anger a couple of times," reminisces Sally. "The psychologist at

87

Bryn Mawr said there was something wrong — either Mike was denying reality or something — because he should have been angry and depressed. Somehow I read this report and said something about it to him. Mike told me he was more interested in getting better and didn't want to expend his energy on being angry.

"Anyway, we got together for a computer session that day and he finally told me that he was angry. We talked about that more than we did the computer that day. But he admitted how the accident had changed his life, and it was hard for him to have to work so hard just to get back to where he was ... whatever other people took for granted, he had to work for so very hard.

"What was unique about our situation was that I had a parent become handicapped so I had seen it as a child watching a parent. Now I could go through it with Mike and I could see the stages from an adult perspective. That was very healing for me."

CHAPTER 11

Recovery Milestones

Speech Milestones

That spring of 1991 I typed a document for my dad on my computer. I got a lot of enjoyment out of doing that type of work, and it got me thinking about doing some volunteer typing at the hospital where I was receiving physical therapy. As I thought about doing volunteer work, I also realized that my speech needed to be polished up first. I talked to my physical therapist about taking speech therapy again, and she told me that I would need to be reevaluated first to determine whether or not it would be beneficial.

On Tuesday, April 23, 1991, I was reevaluated, and my speech therapist informed me that I probably needed adjustments and/or additions to my palatal lift. She also told me she had received a phone call from the dentist who made my palatal lift. He had just designed a hand-held prothesis that would help patients with head injuries and without a voice box become better understood. She invited me to be part of a test group of this new device. I was very interested.

So, on Monday, April 29, 1991, I went to my first

evening class. The dentist familiarized all of us with the hand held prosthesis that we would use during the class. As usual, I was quite a bit harder on myself than the instructor was. I expected to do in one evening what would take five weeks. The following day, I realized that it would take time and would not occur instantaneously. I stayed with it and finished the program on May 30. It helped a lot.

Walking Milestones

During the morning hours of April 15, I began to use my single-point cane solely. Since I didn't have therapy that day, I was able to practice with it at my home. The following day, all day, I used it to walk everywhere! I even used it to walk into the dentist's office. God touched me again!

Regaining Strength

People who aren't familiar with the results of a serious head injury don't realize that making any type of progression is a big deal, and that's one of the reasons that I wrote this story. I had never really thought about my progression, but now I realize I have come quite a long way. As I've said before, "the miracles would still continue." Because I was working on strengthening my leg muscles during my physical therapy, walking with the regular cane was a little easier than when I first began to use the quadcane.

I must have been regaining my strength, because I soon found out how powerful my sneezes were. One day after getting out of the kitchen chair, I sneezed and fell backwards on my butt! "*Brother*," I thought, "*that must*

90

*have been **some sneeze!***"

On May 20, early in the morning, I lost my balance again and fell on my floor. This time I fell forward instead of backward. I didn't have any broken skin or bruises. I believe this was assurance from the Lord that I had nothing to worry about.

I've Come a Long Way!

One of the most exciting parts of my recovery has been for me to go back to visit doctors and nurses who took care of me very early in my recovery. To be able to hear them 'ooh and aah' over how good I look and how far I've come really serves as a faith-builder for me that God, the Master Healer, is always with me. He continues to heal me even when I get discouraged that my progress isn't going fast enough.

That summer I went back to P.G. Hospital and saw some of the Critical Care nurses who cared for me right after my accident. One of the nurses kept saying that I looked so good. It felt quite odd walking back into the same unit where many feared I wouldn't make it out alive.

In June, I called one of the Primary Day Care nurses at BMRH Hospital, and surprisingly, she knew who it was right after I said "*Hello.*" I spoke very clearly to her over the phone.

Two days later, I visited a few of the nurses and therapists at BMRH. My mom and my cousin Carol came along as well and we spent one night at a hotel in Wayne, Pennsylvania. It was exciting to me because I hadn't stayed in a hotel room overnight and alone since the accident. I even had a handicapped accessible bathroom, so I was able to shower standing up using guardrails. Everyone greeted me warmly. I was able to see my physiatrist at BMRH. I was really touched by the fact that people remembered me even after not seeing me for a little over two years. I did remember the names of a few therapists and nurses, but I mainly remembered their faces. My former speech therapist and my early physical therapist, Johanna, talked to me during their lunch break. Johanna introduced me to one of the new physical therapists as "*the famous Michael Peake!*"

Courage & Stamina

I received a letter from my friend Tom Timmes. I was very uplifted because in the letter he told me that, in a sense, I was a role model for him. He said every time he sees me I am improving. In his letter he wrote, "Seeing your courage and stamina helps me get through my struggles. After seeing what you've been through, it makes what I have to deal with much easier." Calling my progress "phenomenal," he relates: "I saw you go from coma to eye movement to spelling out words to moving about in a wheelchair. Now you are getting back your motor skills and talking with the lift and using a single-point cane!"

That summer I went into my back yard *unassisted* with my single-point cane! I entered and exited through stairs located on our deck. It was three years ago on June 16 that my accident happened and, praise God, the miracles continue!

CHAPTER 12

Seizure

July 24, 1991 was a pretty normal day until around 5 p.m. While in my room, I was carrying some slacks to wear to church that evening. As I walked by my bed, I had a seizure; followed shortly by another one. Thank God I was able to fall on my bed when it happened; and also that my mom saw me when I fell. She told me as she looked in on me, my facial skin color and expression changed as I looked up at her; then I took a step back and plopped down on my bed where my body began to shake.

Since something like this had never happened before, my mom didn't know who to call first. She telephoned my physical medicine doctor, Dr. Panagos, but without success. She then dialed "911." The operator was very helpful and gave my mom instructions. She stayed on the phone with her until the ambulance arrived. Mom worried about the palatal lift in my mouth and was told not to try and remove it. She was greatly relieved to find that I didn't have it in my mouth after all.

When my neighbors saw the ambulance in our driveway, they began to worry and wonder. I was unconscious for about half an hour. During that time, I was rushed to Doctor's Hospital in an ambulance with two paramedics and my mom. They took my blood pressure, put a needle in my arm for an IV, took my temperature, and monitored my heart. When I awoke I began to wonder, "*What am I doing in a hospital?*" Thankfully, as when I came out of the first coma, I didn't thrash around. About an hour after I woke up, the lab technician disconnected my heart monitor and gave me a CT scan so that the doctors would be able to tell what caused my seizure. It didn't show anything new. But, much to my surprise, I wasn't going home yet. I was to have a spinal tap performed by a neurologist. She warned me that I couldn't sit up until about eight hours after the spinal tap or else I would get severe headache — a headache that medicine couldn't relieve. I didn't get that headache, but I did get an extremely painful lower backache a little while afterwards.

The pain lasted for about two hours. I needed to stay overnight at the hospital and got only a few hours of sleep. They removed the IV needle and discharged me the following day. I was given an electroencephalogram (EEG) that Friday. It is a painless test performed by having electrodes placed on the head that detect electrical impulses in the brain. It showed that everything was fine and that there was no abnormal activity. The doctor gave me some medicine that would help prevent me from having another seizure, but unfortunately it would help me only while I remained on it. I prayed first, and decided not to take the medication, because it also had side effects. As a result of the seizure, my arm and leg muscles were temporarily weaker.

I resumed using my shower chair until I could restrengthen my muscles. I still ended up with a less severe headache for four days. It seemed to be related to the spinal tap. I found that lying down did relieve it a little

94

and better than any headache medication. I thought that it would just last for a day or two, but I was wrong. Because I had hardly any balance, I needed to use my wheelchair to transport myself around. I tried going to church that Sunday morning in my wheelchair, but I was only able to stay in Sunday School for about 20 minutes. My head really began to ache, so I went home and got some relief by lying down.

A "Doozy" of a Miracle!

I had just finished reading the book entitled *Kathy* [by Barbara Miller and Charles Paul Conn., Fleming H. Revell Co., New York, 1979] right before I had the seizure. It is the story about the miraculous recovery of a head injured patient. On the evening of Monday, July 29, I remembered one chapter of the book where the mother wrote about how she felt that God wanted her to look to Him for support. Scripture came to her one morning; Scripture that spoke of healing found in the New Testament of the Holy Bible. James 5:14-15 describes the Biblical practice of anointing with oil. She found a Bible and read them carefully:

> *"Is there any sick among you? Let him call for the elders of the church: and let them pray over him, anointing him with oil in the name of the Lord: And the prayer of faith shall save the sick, and the Lord shall raise him up...."*

Since I had already seen and believed in the power of prayer, I had my parents anoint me with oil and pray for God to heal me from the headache on the evening of July

29, 1991. As soon as the prayer was completed, the headache went away! Since the headache no longer bothered me, I went a step further. I removed the shower chair from my bathtub Tuesday morning and resumed taking my showers standing up. After the shower, I parked the wheelchair and began to walk with my single-point cane! I walked by faith into therapy with it. I still used the wheelchair during the latter part of the day.

On August 12, 1991, I saw my neurologist. I asked her if she believed in miracles. When she said yes, I told her that I had a "doozy" for her. The miracle that God performed on me was permanently relieving me of the headache. I looked fine and she didn't even reschedule me for a follow-up visit!

During that month, I read another moving book about Josh McDowell called *The Excitement of the Unexpected* by Joe Musser [Here's Life Publishers, Inc., California, 1981]. My Aunt Geneva and Uncle Don had given the book to me for Christmas in 1983. Unfortunately, I wasn't that interested in reading at that time, but now I don't mind reading as much. In the book, examples were given of how Josh prayed to the Lord, and then things that no one expected to occur did! It added to my knowledge that prayer is important in my recovery. Too many unexplainable "coincidences" have occurred in my life to refute that.

A few days after my headache miraculously disappeared, I wrote a "Thank you" letter to Aunt Geneva, Uncle Don, and their church, Rileyville Baptist Church in Virginia, for praying for me. The disappearance of my headache was definitely an answer to prayer! Their church congregation had been praying for me ever since they heard about my accident.

I received a return letter on August 27, 1991, in

which the pastor told me the congregation appreciated my taking the time out to write them. He shared my letter with the whole congregation in their Sunday morning service. He stated that "*a letter such as this helped strengthen the faith of those who were praying. We rejoice with you at the way in which you have experienced God's healing hand upon your life, ...*"

Ever since having the seizure, my palatal lift seemed to be more in the way, so I didn't use it. My speech was understandable without it. During speech therapy on a Tuesday morning early in September, I asked the speech pathologist if I could really focus on trying to talk without the lift. She told me that things looked promising because my breath control and diction had improved since I was reevaluated by her this past April. I believe God caused more good to come from the seizure than bad.

"God is Repairing & Restoring Damage"

"See, you haven't got that thing in your mouth and you're better without it," exclaimed Rev. Handel Price, the evangelist, who prayed with me and my dad while I was in a coma, when I met with him again in September of 1991. "God's doing a work, and that's the thing you've got to be aware of — that God's doing it. It's not just the doctors — the doctors have been marvelous. They've done everything they possibly could. But there is a limit to their ability and there is no limit to God's ability. God can do the impossible. And there's the key — you've been trusting God and God's been bringing you through step by step. And He's going to complete it. He who has started a work will continue it and **will** complete it.

"It's been three years since your accident, Mike. You wouldn't believe you're the same fellow. You were hardly able to speak, you were hardly able to move around, but now you can walk, sometimes unaided now. You see my conviction is this: that God is changing the condition of your brain. He's causing it to react now in areas it hasn't reacted. You see it's something that God's doing. God's repairing all the damage. Places that have been marred because of the accident, God's restoring them and renewing them."

CHAPTER 13

1991: More Improvements

My mom and I went shopping on Friday, August 30, 1991. This time we brought my wheelchair along with us. I was able to fold up the wheelchair, place it in and remove it from our van, and maneuver around the store — unassisted!

During the week of September 1, I was reevaluated for speech therapy **without the lift**. After my speech therapist observed the back of my throat by holding my mouth open with a tongue depressor while I said a few vowels, she said that I sounded a lot better than it had appeared. She couldn't see any movement, but I was still able to make sounds without talking through my nose. When I used to wear the palatal lift, I couldn't make the "s" sound. Now I could! Now that I wasn't using the palatal lift, I needed new speech goals.

I also showed significant improvement when I was given a partial reevaluation in physical therapy. I had improved in areas which might seem insignificant, but each of those areas add to anyone's overall stability and/or balance. I excelled in maintaining my balance with one foot forward, and improved my regular walking and in going up and down stairs.

Look What the Lord Has Done!

On September 16, 1991, I walked, *without* my cane or any supportive device, more than the length of my house — approximately 60 feet. I couldn't believe I could do it until about halfway through my journey. At one point I hollered to my mom, "Hey mom! Guess what I'm doing?" (That's the way I usually am. I try to do something new alone, and if I'm successful, then I reveal myself.)

My mom was babysitting my niece, Rebekah, so she had no idea what I was up to. When she came to the room and saw me, she was ecstatic. We were all thrilled and said "Look what the Lord has done!" I could do it only for a brief amount of time and then I tired out, but hey, it was another beginning!

I had an additional thought on the evening of September 25, 1991 — it's not only nice but important to have any type of therapist treat the patient as a real person, not as a daily routine or part of their job. I thanked my physical therapist the next day for treating me as a real person. That has really made an impact on my progression.

On October 25, 1991, I became an uncle again to Emily Anne Kogok. It has been a good year. God is still bestowing gifts to all our family.

CHAPTER 14

1991-92: Realizations & Reflections

On Friday evening, October 4, 1991, I was really embarrassed and shocked while attending the youth service at my church.

We divided into three teams, each team having to think of a commercial to perform in front of a video camera. Additionally, each team had to make that commercial have spiritual emphasis. Each team went to separate rooms, and, of course, my team had the room farthest to walk to! Since it took me a little longer walking to the meeting room, I left my team a little early so I would not hold up the group. With extra time before my group was to perform, I went into the room. Just messing around, I performed my own little commercial.

What I didn't find out until we viewed all of them was that I was being videotaped. After we watched everyone else's commercials, mine came up. I was shocked at the fact that even I had trouble understanding myself. Additionally, since it was later in the evening, I walked like an old man with my back bending over. To make matters worse, I didn't have the details of the commercial right! Even though the commercials were supposed to be funny, nobody laughed at mine. Maybe nobody wanted me to think they were laughing *at* me. They weren't even able to tell what it was about. I thought that I was doing a lot better than what I had looked like on the videotape.

My physical deficits as a result of my head injury have changed my involvement with the youth group **drastically.** I no longer go on the outings, participate in fundraisers, or plan parties. Many of my friends stay up late and go out in the evening; that's when I tire out. I'm no longer the night owl I used to be. I just attend as many of the meetings as I can. My friendships have changed as well. Friends have either moved away, quit attending my church, gone off to college, or just found themselves busy attending other matters in their lives.

I do realize that many head injury patients do not have any type of support, and that is one of the key ingredients necessary for any patient's recovery. I am thankful to the Lord that my family gives me a lot of the emotional support I need. I have made new friendships as well; many made through therapy, and am thankful to still keep in contact with a few pre-accident friends.

People who are not handicapped need to realize that those of us who are enjoy socializing with people our own age. It is also the handicapped person's responsibility to help initiate social contact, if at all possible.

Another realization hit me on October 13, 1991: I'm not really as old as I legally am. I missed out on my 19th and 20th growing years of my life due to the accident. Those were some of the most important years of my life; the years in which I was beginning to discover just exactly who I was. I am extremely thankful that I know who I am now, but without any choice. I had to start my life at the beginning instead of where I left off! In a few areas of my life, I have no memory as to how to handle them.

More Independence

On November 21, 1991, my physical therapist told me she thought I was ready to go downstairs to the small fitness gym *independently!* This meant that I could walk down the stairs without anyone around, but I would still need to hold onto the railing.

On December 12, 1991, my speech therapist told me the only "medical" reason I sound better without the palatal lift is that I was part of the research held earlier that year in May. Notice how she said medical, leaving room for other reasons — maybe she, too, realized it was God.

Another Seizure

On January 4, 1992, I suffered another seizure while I was in my bathroom. My mom told me that while she was in the hallway outside my room, she heard a loud "bang" come from my bathroom. She came into my room, opened my bathroom door and found me lying on the bathroom floor. Thank God I didn't hit my head on the bathroom sink, which was very close by. I don't remember what I was doing before I had it. I had three in total, lasting from 2.5 to 12.5 minutes each. I was scheduled to have a youth party at my house that evening. I still went ahead with a short party because I felt all right afterward.

Anti-Seizure Medicine

On January 7, 1992, a second neurologist started me on a medicine called dilantin to keep me from having more seizures. Some of the side effects of this medicine, such as drowsiness and loss of balance, really began to impair the rate of my recovery.

Because of this, my neurologist wanted to start me on a new medication called tegretol on February 12, 1992. My parents and I were wary of the possible side effects of the tegretol, which include damage to the immune system — a concern when one doesn't have a spleen. But after consultation with Dr. Panagos, my physical medicine doctor, we decided I should take it. So, three days later, I began taking one tablet of tegretol along with my regular dosage of dilantin. I gradually increased to twice daily and then to three times daily. As soon as I was taking the tegretol three times a day, the dilantin dosage was diminished two days later. It took about one month to get the dilantin totally out of my system.

Since the dilantin was affecting my balance, coordination and other visible physical attributes, my physical therapist gave me a three-week break from physical therapy. The break started February 24, 1992 and resumed on March 16, 1992. However, I continued taking speech therapy over the break.

From January 4, 1992, the date of the seizure, until March 3, 1992, I had been using my wheelchair to make my overnight trips to the bathroom. From March 4 until my birthday on March 7, I tried using just my single-point cane for those journeys. I was successful! On March 7, however, I *almost* fell but didn't.

I believe this was God telling me that yes, I have been healed from the seizure, but will have obstacles to overcome. As long as my family and I keep our trust in the Lord, we will make it through any setbacks.

"The Lord has done so much," reflects Mike's sister, Karen. "I guess the toughest thing now is not to take what He has done for granted. Even His blessings can begin to numb you after a while, and I know I have to guard against that.

"Every new day for Mike can be considered a miracle since he had such a slim chance at life and recovery at all. I need to make that my personal thought for each day."

EPILOGUE

A Typical Day

Today, over five years after the accident, a fairly typical day for me begins around 6 a.m. I shower independently, dress and shave myself. I then prepare breakfast. After eating I make my bed, then either exercise or work on things at my desk and computer. I go to physical therapy two days a week. Two to three mornings I put in a load of laundry before preparing breakfast.

The days I go to therapy I often eat lunch out. When I get home, I either nap or finish my exercises. After dinner we read the Bible as a family then play games. I usually go to bed around 9 p.m.

Mom's Reflections

It has been over five years since the day of Mike's accident and his life was drastically changed. I have never asked any of the nurses or doctors how far they felt Mike would recover because I had placed him in God's hands since the accident. I felt if He kept him alive that He would help him recover completely because He had a plan for Mike's life. If He chose to save him, I felt He would use Mike's life to touch others for Him.

When Michael was discharged from the Rehab Hospital, his physical therapist felt he would always need a wheelchair out in the community but he would probably be able to get around the house with a walker. The psychologist felt he would lose motivation to improve and be depressed. Mike's speech therapist felt he would always have speech deficits and most people would have trouble understanding him.

Setbacks like seizures have occurred, but milestones have been reached as well. Between Michael's first and second seizure, he has been able to walk through the house without his cane for a short period of time. It takes more energy and his back muscles need to become stronger. We believe he is going to get his balance and strength back to walk all the time without his cane. We wait upon the Lord to strengthen and continually heal Michael in His time.

God is faithful and is there for each one of us each minute as we call out to Him whether it be for strength, courage, inner peace, wisdom to make decisions or protection as we commit our lives to Him and seek His will.

Michael has learned to do this. Jesus has taken away the fear he had of falling as well as giving him a peace within his soul. Each day is a new adventure to discover what God has in store for us and how we can be of service to Him. No matter what happens, our hope lives in our relationship with Jesus Christ and the day we will meet him face to face.

Even though I believe God did not cause the

accident, I believe that God allowed it to happen. I also believe that good can come out of every tragedy that happens to us if we allow God to use us and share with others how He has blessed our lives.

God has been with Mike literally every step of the way and I know He will continue to meet his needs and be there as we daily walk with Him.

TRAUMATIC CLOSED HEAD INJURY

*General Information

According to the National Head Injury Foundation, there are over 2 million traumatic brain injuries in the United States per year, with 500,000 severe enough to require hospital admission.

Every 15 seconds, someone receives a head injury in the United States; every five minutes one of these people will die and others will become permanently disabled.

Young men between the ages of 15 and 24 have the highest rate of injury. Motor vehicle crashes cause one-half of all traumatic brain injuries, with falls accounting for 21%, assaults and violence 12%, and sports and recreation accidents 10%.

Each year 75,000 to 100,000 Americans will die as a result of a traumatic brain injury. Most deaths occur at the time of injury or within the first two hours of hospitalization. Of those who survive, each year, approximately 70,000 to 90,000 will endure life-long debilitating loss of function. An additional 2,000 will exist in a persistent vegetative state.

How the Brain Works

The brain is the control center not only for all body movement and sensation, but also for how a person thinks, acts and feels. The brain is one part of the central nervous system and coordinates the thought processes and movements, receives messages from the sensory organs, interprets the messages and formulates responses to them. These responses are then sent to various centers of the body resulting in speech, body movements, and general body functioning. Damage to the brain threatens the well-being of the individual by interrupting these processes.

Serious traumatic head injury is one of the common threats to normal brain function. It can occur when the head hits something, for example, during a motor vehicle, bicycle, skateboard, or roller skate accident. A closed head injury is one in which there has not been any penetration of the skull.

The brain is protected from such injury by a group of bones which are tightly joined together to make up the skull or cranium. The bones of the skull (cranium) completely enclose both the brain and the spinal fluid (cerebrospinal fluid) in which the brain floats. The lower end of the brain (brain stem) is not free to move. The many cranial nerves which leave the brain stem play a part in securing it to the base of the head. It is difficult to determine the degree and type of injury.

Brain Injury

Each patient with a brain trauma has had a different injury. This is extremely important to understand because one cannot compare the amount or rate of recovery of two patients without considering the severity and nature of the underlying damage.

To understand why there are multiple sites of injury, picture a glass jar filled with water in which you have a rubber ball almost as large as the jar. When the jar is at rest, the ball floats in the center. When the jar is suddenly pushed forward, the ball hits the back of the jar. When the jar's movement is suddenly stopped, the ball continues forward until it is stopped by the front of the jar, where it bounces back again and hits the back, and again forward. This backward and forward movement continues until the ball again comes to rest in the center.

In traumatic brain injury, a similar sequence of events happens as the brain rebounds off the inside of the skull producing multiple places of injury in the process. This makes it difficult to predict accurately the extent and type of damage, or the possible outcome. Each traumatic head injury can be expected to produce a unique set of brain injuries and problems.

MAJOR TYPES OF BRAIN INJURIES

Several types of brain injuries are common either alone or in combinations.

1.   **Diffuse axonal injury** is a widespread microscopic injury to nerve connections (axons) along with injury to specific brain structures including the upper brain stem.

2.   **Focal injury** or damage to a specific area of the brain can occur in several ways:

      a.   Bruising of an area of the brain (**contusion**).

      b.   Bleeding within the brain (**intracerebral hemorrhage**).

      c.   Loss of blood supply to a part of the brain (**infarction**).

111

3.   **Bleeding**
      a.   **Epidural hematoma** is a blood clot outside the brain and its lining membrane, the dura; problems are usually the result of compression of the underlying brain, especially the brain stem.
      b.   **Subdural hematoma** is a blood clot overlying the brain and underneath the lining membrane, the dura; there is often associated contusion; problems are most severe when the brain stem is compressed by pressure from the overlying hematoma.
4.   **Anoxic brain injury** is an interruption of the amount of oxygen reaching the brain, resulting in brain cell damage.
5.   **Cerebral aneurysms** are sac-like dilatations in the wall of an artery in the brain and are caused by weaknesses in the vessel wall.
6.   **Brain tumors** are collections of abnormal cells which grow at different rates within the skull.
7.   **Brain stem injury** is an injury to a part of the brain which can affect such things as movement, muscle tone, consciousness, and eye movements.

Coma

As a result of traumatic head injury, the person may become unconscious. When the loss of consciousness lasts for more than a brief period, the patient is considered to be in a coma. Coma results from a disruption of nerve fibers going to the brain stem. The word "coma" is used to describe a loss of consciousness in which the patient does not open his eyes, does not speak, and does not follow commands. There is a total absence of awareness, even when he is externally stimulated. Between consciousness and coma there are a variety of altered states of

112

consciousness.

The neurosurgeon can judge the seriousness of a closed head injury by evaluating the depth of coma, using clinical neurologic signs (Glasgow Coma Scale), CT Scans and other specialized tests. It takes an xray-like picture of slices of the brain and is used to observe for damage. Although CT scans have been a major advance in medical care, they may not always reflect the true extent of the damage, and may even look normal in the face of severe disabling injury.

Physicians tend to be very pessimistic when talking to families about likely outcome as they do not wish to raise false hopes. Physicians must consider the statistical likelihood or the odds that a certain course of events will occur, whereas an individual patient may have a much different outcome.

When deep coma persists, the chances are only 50-50 that the patient will survive even with the best medical care. However, once the medical situation stabilizes over the first week or two, the chances are excellent that the individual will live.

Predicting long-term outcome and degree of disability after serious head injury is much more difficult. It is true that the longer a coma lasts, the greater the disability is likely to be. The prognosis for a child with a closed head injury is considerably better than that for an adult. Even after prolonged coma lasting six weeks, good recovery can be expected in most.

Stages of Coma Recovery (Rancho Level Scale)

Level I: **No Response**
The patient appears to be in deep sleep and is not responsive to light, sound, voice, pain or touch.

113

Level II: **Generalized Response**

The patient is beginning to show signs of waking up. He reacts to deep pain (pinch). You may see the patient move around, open his eyes; however, he does not do this when asked.

Level III: **Localized Response**

At times, the patient is able to follow simple directions, like "close your eyes," or "squeeze my hand." It may take the patient a long time to follow the direction and the patient may not do it at all. The patient may become more aware of his body and may do one or more of these things: pull at his nasogastric tube, pull at his catheter, pull at his arm/leg restraints.

Level IV: **Confused-Agitated**

The patient may be more active than before. He may be moving constantly, so restraints may be necessary to prevent injury. Attention is poor. The patient may be unable to cooperate when asked to follow directions. You may see the following behavior: flailing motions, screaming or crying out, aggression, attempt to remove restraints or tubes, trying to get out of bed.

The patient will need more help with feeding, dressing, washing and may be able to sit and walk, but not always safely and not always when asked. The patient may not always remember where he is, who you are, and what happened to him; even if you just told him. He may be talking, but not always making sense.

Level V: **Confused Inappropriate, non-agitated**

The patient appears much calmer. He is able to follow one-step directions and answer simple questions most of the time. If you ask too much, too fast, the patient will show signs of frustration. Attention has improved, but the patient can only attend to one thing or persons for a short time. He is easily distracted by the television, radio, movement in the hall or room, and other conversations.

The patient needs less help with feeding, dressing, washing, but may need to be reminded to start and to continue until he is done. The patient does better remembering information from before the injury, but is not able to remember things that have happened since the injury. He may not use familiar objects correctly unless he is shown. The patient's speech may sound "robot-like" and may not always be appropriate to the conversation/situation.

Level VI: Confused-Appropriate

The patient follows simple directions consistently and is able to do common daily activities like bathing, putting on a shirt, combing hair. He is able to remember more about events before his accident; however, he still has trouble remembering things that he has been told since the accident.

The patient is more aware of making mistakes and may get angry at himself or others when the mistakes happen. The patient still needs help from others to know what to do and when to do it.

Level VII: Automatic-Appropriate

The patient may look like he can complete common daily activities by himself, but needs to have someone there at all times to be sure he is safe. The patient will take more time to learn things over again. Patient believes he can do all the things he did before his accident including driving his car (BUT HE CAN'T).

The patient may be able to have a short conversation, but has more trouble with long conversations that require making conclusions, making a judgment, making plans, knowing right from wrong, and listening to more than one person.

Level VIII: Purposeful-Appropriate

The patient is independent in his common daily

activities.   He is now ready to be seen by vocation rehabilitation to see what kind of work he can do.

He is now able to learn new information and to use it with old information to: make conclusions, make a judgment, make plans, know right from wrong, and follow conversations with more than one person.

Rehabilitation and Prognosis

Rehabilitation for brain injury is still in the early stages of development.   An important part of any rehabilitation program is a supportive family with abundant patience. It is important to remember that the patient will rapidly become mentally and physically tired. Pushing the patient beyond reason will not speed learning.

Since the brain is unable to regenerate itself like other body tissue, brain retraining techniques are gaining increasing support.   This technique begins with the assumption that there is considerable duplication of the various parts of the brain that enable it to perform complex tasks.   Hence, if one part is destroyed, the brain could possibly be trained to use another part through simplified educational approaches.

According to the Maryland Head Injury Foundation "Guidebook on Head Injury," the following are **possible effects on behavior, thinking, physical abilities and emotions from the brain injury** suffered by the head injured.

BEHAVIOR CHANGES

Agitation.   The patient may be restless, upset, even combative toward family members or hospital personnel.   These are commonly observed symptoms, which are not fully understood but may express the irritability of the newly healing brain. The nerve pathways have been disrupted, and the patient may have difficulty processing information and reacting to stimuli.

Distractibility. Brain injury may make it harder to sort out important stimuli from useless information coming in from the environment. A noisy or busy or complicated environment distracts the patient and makes it more difficult to concentrate. Simple, peaceful situations are better.

Emotional Lability. The recoveree may tend to be a grouch: impatient, easily annoyed by trivial upsets. The world is harder for the patient to understand and control. Frequent frustration is the result.

Obsessing. The opposite of distractibility: the patient may fix on a thought and not be able to get off of it. This is partly due to memory loss.

Reaction time. The patient may seem to be living in slow motion. Speech, movement and reaction to stimulation all take longer.

Self-centeredness. The patient may develop a lessened concern for others' needs since it takes so much energy to cope with his or her own changed self and situation.

Sexual Behavior. Brain injury may lead to loss of sexual interest, sexual hyperactivity, lack of inhibition, or altered sexual behavior patterns.

Social Inappropriateness. There may be impulsivity, acting quickly on thoughts without filtering them for appropriateness, resulting in actions or speech that may embarrass family members.

PROBLEMS OF THINKING/COGNITION

The head injured patient may have problems in **abstraction**, the ability to "read between the lines;" **aphasia**, in which the patient no longer can match the name of something with the actual object; **anomia**, in which he has difficulty in recalling nouns or names. Other problems include: **aphonia**, the loss of ability to speak using normal voice; **apraxia**, the inability to do something voluntarily that can be done automatically; **confabulation**, elicitation of imaginary things and events to fill in for lapses in memory. This is not lying; it is an attempt to make sense of poor memory. The head injured patient may also have problems with: **limited attention span, difficulty in concentration, denial of deficits, discrimination, disorientation, judgment, memory, organization, perseveration, problem solving and tangential speech.**

PHYSICAL PROBLEMS

The head injured may experience: **breathing difficulty, chewing and swallowing difficulties, fatigue, hearing and vision problems, insatiable drive for food or liquid, motor deficits, perceptual deficits, regulatory disturbances,** and **dysarthria**, a collection of speech problems that stem from muscle weakness or paralysis affecting the patient's ability to communicate effectively.

Some **COMMON EMOTIONAL PROBLEMS** that a kind and understanding attitude of family members can help the recoveree deal with are:

Loss of Self-Image: A person's concept of self is made up of vocation and other activities, appearance,

118

abilities, manner of speaking, long-term plans — and in a second all that is gone. The patient has to develop a new "self" from scratch. Appearance, abilities and plans may now have characteristics the patient used to think of as bad, worthless or useless. Competitive, judgmental attitudes of both patient and family have to change to include the injured person as just as valued as before, though changed.

Major Role Changes:

Since head injury so often happens to a young person (a person in late adolescence) who has been trying to free himself from the dependency of childhood into the independence of adulthood, he can be discouraged as he is suddenly dependent on his parents again. This is naturally very upsetting and discouraging. Treating the patient as if he or she has the same role as before the injury, even if only in little ways, can ease the shock of a major role change.

Sometimes head injuries happen later in life to people who already have their careers, education and family. All of a sudden their skills that they worked so hard to achieve are taken away from them. There is naturally anger over being forced into this situation. Now the person must reevaluate what skills they do have and change the direction of their career.

Mourning:

If other people were killed or seriously injured in the incident that injured the patient, guilt and grief may have to be worked through.

Loss of Friends:

This is a very common problem for the head injured and tends to result in anger by family members against friends who do not "stick by" the patient in time of trouble. Perhaps the anger results from a misunderstanding of the nature of friendship. Friendship is a condition nourished by shared activities. There are no longer the same shared activities, so the friendships fade. Late adolescence, when most head injuries occur, is a time of rapid "sampling" of people to learn about the world and life. Friendships may be of shorter duration than later and thus less stable. The answer is the same as would have occurred without the injury: make new friends of the people who are in the new situations. However, the falling away of old friends may be very sad for the patient. It is helpful if the family can facilitate even occasional visits. This provides a transition for the patient and minimizes feelings of rejection.

No one knows for certain what the **final degree of recovery** will be after a brain injury. However, these are some useful guidelines:

1.   Significant recovery can occur even after severe brain injuries.
2.   Severe confusion is common soon after injury and can be temporary.
3.   No one can reliably quote a period of time in which recovery stops. Many patients have continued to show progress for several years.
4.   Sometimes, although progress is occurring, the rate can be frustratingly slow. Rapid change is most likely in the first few months after injury.
5.   In severe brain injuries, even after significant recovery, residual problems almost always remain. Frequently problems with personality, concentration, memory, problem solving, temper control, headaches, or depression continue even when physical problems are no

longer noticeable. In other patients, problems with walking, speech, vision, or coordination may be more persistent. Many patients recover to the point of leading full and meaningful lives. However, roles and relationships are frequently changed.

6. The best estimates for recovery are done on an individual basis and with an understanding of the type and extent of injury, as well as prior personal characteristics.

Where to go for Information on Rehabilitation

There are a number of services to which you can turn for guidance. Your doctor, physical therapist and rehabilitation facility is the best place to turn for information on your specific case. Here are some others:

1. Your State Department of Rehabilitation
2. Your local school system
3. The Easter Seal Society in your community
4. Professional schools for occupational and physical therapy in or near your community
5. Community hospitals

Gather as much knowledge as possible about the services within your community to allow you to make a decision which will best meet the patient's needs.

And don't ever forget: "For with God nothing is impossible." Luke 1:37

SOURCES OF INFORMATION:

"Coma After Traumatic Head Injury: A Guide for Families," Prepared by the **National Head Injury Foundation**, January 1983, 18A Vernon Street, Framingham, MA 01701, (617) 879-7473;

"A Family Brochure for the Closed Head Injured Adult," **Maryland Head Injury, Foundation, Inc;**

"Guidebook on Head Injury," **Maryland Head Injury Foundation, Inc.**, 1990, 916 S. Rolling Rd., Catonsville, MD 21228, 800-221-MHIF;

"Head Injury," by Lawrence F. Marshall, M.D., Georgia Robins Sadler, M.B.A., Sharon Bowers Marshall, B.S.N., The Comprehensive Central Nervous System Injury Center for San Diego County, 1981, **The Central Nervous System Injury Foundation**, 4050 Front Street, San Diego, CA 92103;

"Brain Injury Family Guide," 1987, by **Bryn Mawr Rehabilitation Hospital Brain Injury Committee**, 414 Paoli Pike, Malvern, PA 19355, (215) 251-5400.

124